A THEOLOGY
FOR THE SOCIAL GOSPEL

WALTER RAUSCHENBUSCH

A THEOLOGY
FOR THE
SOCIAL GOSPEL

Abingdon Press

NASHVILLE

A THEOLOGY FOR THE SOCIAL GOSPEL

Copyright renewal 1945 by Pauline E. Rauschenbusch

Published by The Macmillan Co., 1917
Abingdon reprint edition 1978

Latest printing 1987

ISBN 0-687-41580-2

MANUFACTURED BY THE PARTHENON PRESS AT
NASHVILLE, TENNESSEE, UNITED STATES OF AMERICA

FOREWORD

In April, 1917, I had the honour of delivering four lectures on the Nathaniel W. Taylor Foundation before the Annual Convocation of the Yale School of Religion. These lectures are herewith presented in elaborated form.

The Taylor Lectures are expected to deal with some theme in Doctrinal Theology, but the Faculty in their invitation indicated that a discussion of some phase of the social problem would be welcome. I have tried to obey this suggestion and still to remain well within the original purpose of the Foundation by taking as my subject, " A Theology for the Social Gospel."

Of my qualifications for this subject I have reason to think modestly, for I am not a doctrinal theologian either by professional training or by personal habits of mind. Professional duty and intellectual liking have made me a teacher of Church History, and the events of my life, interpreted by my religious experiences, have laid the social problems on my mind. On the other hand, it may be that the necessity of approaching systematic theology from the outside may be of real advantage. Theology has often received its most fruitful impulses when secular life and movements have set it new problems.

Of the subject itself I have no cause to speak modestly. Its consideration is of the highest importance for the future of theology and religion. It bristles with intellectual problems. This book had to be written some time, and as far as I know, nobody has yet written it. I offer my attempt until some other man comes along who can plough deeper and straighter.

I wish to assure the reader who hesitates in the vestibule, that the purpose of this book is wholly positive and constructive. It is just as orthodox as the Gospel would allow. I have dedicated it to an eminent representative of the older theology in order to express my deep gratitude for what I have received from it, and to clasp hands through him with all whose thought has been formed by Jesus Christ.

My fraternal thanks are due to my friends, Professor James Bishop Thomas, Ph.D., of the University of the South, and Professor F. W. C. Meyer of Rochester Theological Seminary, who have given a critical reading to my manuscript and have made valuable suggestions.

CONTENTS

A THEOLOGY FOR THE SOCIAL GOSPEL

CHAPTER I

THE CHALLENGE OF THE SOCIAL GOSPEL TO THEOLOGY

WE have a social gospel. We need a systematic theology large enough to match it and vital enough to back it. This is the main proposition of this book. The first three chapters are to show that a readjustment and expansion of theology, so that it will furnish an adequate intellectual basis for the social gospel, is necessary, feasible, desirable, and legitimate. The remainder of the book offers concrete suggestions how some of the most important sections of doctrinal theology may be expanded and readjusted to make room for the religious convictions summed up in " the social gospel."

Some of my readers, who know the age, the tenacity, and the monumental character of theology well, will smile at the audacity of this proposal. Others, who know theology still better, will treat this venture very seriously. [If theology stops growing or is unable to adjust itself to its modern environment and to meet its present tasks, it will die. Many now regard it as dead. The social gospel needs a theology to make it effective; but theology needs the social gospel to vitalize it. / The work attempted in this book is doomed to futility if it has only the personal ideas of the author behind it. It is worthy of consideration only if the needs of a new epoch are seeking expression in it, and in that case its personal defects are of slight importance.

The argument of this book is built on the conviction that the social gospel is a permanent addition to our spiritual outlook and that its arrival constitutes a stage in the development of the Christian religion.

We need not waste words to prove that the social gospel is being preached. It is no longer a prophetic and occasional note. It is a novelty only in backward social or religious communities. The social gospel has become orthodox.

It is not only preached. It has set new problems for local church work, and has turned the pastoral and organizing work of the ministry into new and constructive directions. It has imparted a wider vision and a more statesmanlike grasp to the foreign mission enterprise. In home missions its advent was signalized by the publication, in 1885, of " Our Country " by Josiah Strong. (*Venerabile nomen!*)   That book lifted the entire home mission problem to a higher level. The religious literature uttering the social gospel is notable both for its volume and its vitality and conviction. The emotional fervour of the new convictions has created prayers and hymns of social aspiration, for which the newer hymn books are making room. Conservative denominations have formally committed themselves to the fundamental ideas of the social gospel and their practical application.

The plans of great interdenominational organizations are inspired by it. It has become a constructive force in American politics.

This new orientation, which is observable in all parts of our religious life, is not simply a prudent adjustment of church methods to changed conditions. There is religious compulsion behind it. Those who are in touch with the student population know what the impulse to social service means to college men and women. It is the most religious element in the life of many of them. Among ministerial students there is an almost impatient demand for a proper social outlet. Some hesitate to enter the regular ministry at all because they doubt whether it will offer them sufficient opportunity and freedom to utter and apply their social convictions. For many ministers who have come under the influence of the social gospel in mature years, it has signified a religious crisis, and where it has been met successfully, it has brought fresh joy and power, and a distinct enlargement of mind. It has taken the place of conventional religion in the lives of many outside the Church. It constitutes the moral power in the propaganda of Socialism.

All those social groups which distinctly face toward the future, clearly show their need and craving for a social interpretation and application of Christianity. Whoever wants to hold audiences of working people must establish some connection between religion and their social feelings and experiences. The religious organizations dealing with college men and women know that any appeal which leaves out the social note is likely to meet a listless audience. The most effective evangelists for these two groups are men who have thoroughly embodied the social gospel in their religious life and thought. When the great evangelistic effort of the " Men and Religion Forward Movement " was first planned, its organizers made room for " Social Service " very hesitatingly. But as soon as the movement was tried out before the public, it became clear that only the meetings which offered the people the social application of religion were striking fire and drawing crowds.

The Great War has dwarfed and submerged all other issues, including our social problems. But in fact the war is the most acute and tremendous social problem of all. All whose Christianity has not been ditched by the catastrophe are demanding a christianizing of international relations. The demand for disarmament and permanent peace, for the rights of the small nations against the imperialistic and colonizing powers, for freedom of the seas and of trade routes, for orderly settlement of grievances,— these are demands for social righteousness and fraternity on the largest scale. Before the War the social gospel dealt with social classes; to-day it is being translated into international terms. The ultimate cause of the war was the same lust for easy and unearned gain which has created the internal social evils under which every nation has suffered. The social problem and the war problem are fundamentally one problem, and the social gospel faces both. After the War the social gospel will " come back " with pent-up energy and clearer knowledge.

The social movement is the most important ethical and spiritual movement in the modern world, and the social gospel is the response of the Christian consciousness to it. Therefore it had to be. The social gospel registers the fact that for the first time in history the spirit of Christianity has had a chance to form a working partnership with real social and psychological science. It is the religious reaction on the historic advent of democracy. It seeks to put the democratic spirit, which the Church inherited from Jesus and the prophets, once more in control of the institutions and teachings of the Church.[1]

The social gospel is the old message of salvation, but enlarged and intensified. The individualistic gospel has taught us to see the sinfulness of every human heart and has inspired us with faith in the willingness and power of God to save every soul that comes to him. But it has not given us an adequate understanding of the sinfulness of the social order and its share in the sins of all individuals within it. It has not evoked faith in the will and power of God to redeem the permanent institutions of human society from their inherited guilt of oppression and extortion. Both our sense of sin and our faith in salvation have fallen short of the realities under its teaching. The social gospel seeks to bring men under repentance for their collective sins and to create a more sensitive and more modern conscience. It calls on us for the

---

[1] In his "Social Idealism and the Changing Theology," embodying the Taylor Lectures for 1912, Professor Gerald B. Smith has shown clearly the discrepancy created by the aristocratic attitude of authority in theology and the spread of democracy in modern ethical life, and has insisted that a readjustment is necessary in theology at this point to conform it to our ethical ideals. Professor Smith expresses the fear that our critical methods by themselves will lead only to a barren intellectualism. That feeling has been one motive in the writing of the present book.

faith of the old prophets who believed in the salvation
of nations.

Now, if this insight and religious outlook become common to large and vigorous sections of the Christian
Church, the solutions of life contained in the old theological system will seem puny and inadequate. Our faith
will be larger than the intellectual system which subtends
it. Can theology expand to meet the growth of faith?
The biblical studies have responded to the spiritual hunger aroused by the social gospel. The historical interpretation of the Bible has put the religious personalities,
their spiritual struggles, their growth, and their utterances, into social connection with the community life of
which they were part. This method of interpretation
has given back the Bible to men of modernized intelligence and has made it the feeder of faith in the social
gospel. The studies of " practical theology " are all in a
process of rejuvenation and expansion in order to create
competent leadership for the Church, and most of these
changes are due to the rise of new ideals created by the
social gospel. What, then, will doctrinal theology do to
meet the new situation? Can it ground and anchor the
social gospel in the eternal truths of our religion and
build its main ideas into the systematic structure of christian doctrine?

Theology is not superior to the gospel. It exists to
aid the preaching of salvation. Its business is to make
the essential facts and principles of Christianity so simple
and clear, so adequate and mighty, that all who preach
or teach the gospel, both ministers and laymen, can draw

on its stores and deliver a complete and unclouded Christian message. When the progress of humanity creates new tasks, such as world-wide missions, or new problems, such as the social problem, theology must connect these with the old fundamentals of our faith and make them Christian tasks and problems.

The adjustment of the Christian message to the regeneration of the social order is plainly one of the most difficult tasks ever laid on the intellect of religious leaders. The pioneers of the social gospel have had a hard time trying to consolidate their old faith and their new aim. Some have lost their faith; others have come out of the struggle with crippled formulations of truth. Does not our traditional theology deserve some of the blame for this spiritual wastage because it left these men without spiritual support and allowed them to become the vicarious victims of our theological inefficiency? If our theology is silent on social salvation, we compel college men and women, workingmen, and theological students, to choose between an unsocial system of theology and an irreligious system of social salvation. It is not hard to predict the outcome. If we seek to keep Christian doctrine unchanged, we shall ensure its abandonment.

Instead of being an aid in the development of the social gospel, systematic theology has often been a real clog. When a minister speaks to his people about child labour or the exploitation of the lowly by the strong; when he insists on adequate food, education, recreation, and a really human opportunity for all, there is response. People are moved by plain human feeling and by the instinctive convictions which they have learned from Jesus

Christ.   But at once there are doubting and dissenting
voices.   We are told that environment has no saving
power; regeneration is what men need; we can not have a
regenerate society without regenerate individuals; we do
not live for this world but for the life to come; it is not
the function of the church to deal with economic questions; any effort to change the social order before the
coming of the Lord is foredoomed to failure.   These objections all issue from the theological consciousness created by traditional church teaching.   These half-truths
are the proper product of a half-way system of theology
in which there is no room for social redemption.   Thus
the Church is halting between two voices that call it.   On
the one side is the voice of the living Christ amid living
men to-day; on the other side is the voice of past ages
embodied in theology.   Who will say that the authority
of this voice has never confused our Christian judgment
and paralysed our determination to establish God's kingdom on earth?

Those who have gone through the struggle for a clear
faith in the social gospel would probably agree that the
doctrinal theology in which they were brought up, was
one of the most baffling hindrances in their spiritual crisis,
and that all their mental energies were taxed to overcome the weight of its traditions.   They were fortunate
if they promptly discovered some recent theological book
which showed them at least the possibility of conceiving
Christian doctrine in social terms, and made them conscious of a fellowship of faith in their climb toward
the light.   The situation would be much worse if Christian thought were nourished on doctrine only.   Fortu-

nately our hymns and prayers have a richer consciousness of solidarity than individualistic theology. But even to-day many ministers have a kind of dumb-bell system of thought, with the social gospel at one end and individual salvation at the other end, and an attenuated connection between them. The strength of our faith is in its unity. Religion wants wholeness of life. We need a rounded system of doctrine large enough to take in all our spiritual interests.

In short, we need a theology large enough to contain the social gospel, and alive and productive enough not to hamper it.

CHAPTER II

THE DIFFICULTIES OF THEOLOGICAL READJUSTMENT

ANY demand for changes in Christian doctrine is sure to cause a quiver of apprehension and distress. Religious truth is the truth our souls live by and it is too dear to be scrapped and made over. Even to grant the possibility of the need of change means a loss of assurance and certitude, and that hurts. The passionate interest of many in the beliefs which have been the food of their spiritual life for years creates a social resistance to change in religious thought. Every generation tries to put its doctrine on a high shelf where the children can not reach it. For instance, the Methodist Church will not be charged with sitting on the clock, but its creed has been put beyond the reach even of the highest body of the Church. Its " Articles of Religion " were an adaptation of the Thirty Nine Articles of the Church of England by John Wesley; to-day they seem to have the better of the starry universe, for they can never change: " The General Conference shall not revoke, alter, nor change our Articles of Religion, nor establish any new standards or rules of doctrine contrary to our present existing and established standards of doctrine."

I have entire sympathy with the conservative instinct which shrinks from giving up any of the dear possessions which have made life holy for us. We have none too much of them left. It is a comfort to me to know that the changes required to make room for the social gospel are not destructive but constructive. They involve addition and not subtraction. The social gospel calls for an expansion in the scope of salvation and for more religious dynamic to do the work of God. It requires more faith and not less. It offers a more thorough and durable salvation. It is able to create a more searching sense of sin and to preach repentance to the respectable and mighty who have ridden humanity to the mouth of hell.

The attacks on our inherited theology have usually come from the intellectuals who are galled by the yoke of uncritical and unhistorical beliefs brought down from pre-scientific centuries. They are entirely within their right in insisting that what is scientifically impossible shall not be laid as an obligatory belief on the neck of modern men in the name of religion. But the rational subtractions of liberalism do not necessarily make religion more religious. We have to snuff the candle to remove the burnt-out wick, but we may snuff out the flame, and all the matches may prove to be damp. Critical clarifying is decidedly necessary, but power in religion comes only through the consciousness of a great elementary need *Schl?* which compels men to lay hold of God anew. The social gospel speaks to such a need, and where a real harmony has been established it has put new fire and power into the old faith.

The power of conservatism is not all due to religious tenderness and loyalty. Some of it results from less worthy causes. Doctrinal theology is in less direct contact with facts than other theological studies. Exegesis and church history deal with historical material and their business is to discover the facts. New facts and the pressure of secular scientific work compel them to revise their results and keep close to realities. Doctrinal theology deals with less substantial and ascertainable things. It perpetuates an esoteric stream of tradition. What every church demands of its systematic theologians is to formulate clearly and persuasively what that church has always held and taught. If they go beyond that they are performing a work of supererogation for which they do not always receive thanks.

Theoretically the Church is the great organization of unselfish service. Actually the Church has always been profoundly concerned for its own power and authority. But its authority rests in large part on the stability of its doctrine. The Roman Catholic Church has always been in the nature of a defensive organization to maintain uniformity of teaching. The physical suppression of heresy was merely the last and crudest means employed by it to resist change. The more subtle and spiritual forms of pressure have doubtless been felt by every person who ever differed with his own church, whatever it was. This selfish ecclesiastical conservatism is not for the Kingdom of God but against it.

Theology needs periodical rejuvenation. Its greatest danger is not mutilation but senility. It is strong and vital when it expresses in large reasonings what youthful religion feels and thinks. When people have to be indoctrinated laboriously in order to understand theology at all, it becomes a dead burden. The dogmas and theological ideas of the early Church were those ideas which at that time were needed to hold the Church together, to rally its forces, and to give it victorious energy against antagonistic powers. To-day many of those ideas are without present significance. Our reverence for them is a kind of ancestor worship. To hold laboriously to a religious belief which does not hold us, is an attenuated form of asceticism; we chastise and starve our intellect to sanctify it by holy beliefs. The social gospel does not need the aid of church authority to get hold of our hearts. It gets hold in spite of such authority when necessary. It will do for us what the Nicene theology did in the fourth century, and the Reformation theology in the sixteenth. Without it theology will inevitably become more and more a reminiscence.[1]

The great religious thinkers who created theology were always leaders who were shaping ideas to meet actual situations. The new theology of Paul was a product of fresh religious experience and of practical necessities. His idea that the Jewish law had been abrogated by Christ's death was worked out in order to set his mission to the Gentiles free from the crippling grip of the past and to make an international religion of Christianity. Luther worked out the doctrine of " justification by faith " because he had found by experience that it gave

[1] President H. C. King's " Reconstruction in Theology " gives an admirable summary of the causes for dissatisfaction with the old doctrinal statements, and of the fundamental moral and spiritual convictions which demand embodiment in theology. See also Prof. Gerald B. Smith's lucid analysis in his " Social Idealism and the Changing Theology."

him a surer and happier way to God than the effort to win merit by his own works.   But that doctrine became the foundation of a new theology for whole nations because it proved to be the battle-cry of a great social and religious upheaval and the effective means of breaking down the semi-political power of the clergy, of shutting up monasteries, of secularizing church property, and of increasing the economic and political power of city councils and princes.   There is nothing else in sight to-day which has power to rejuvenate theology except the consciousness of vast sins and sufferings, and the longing for righteousness and a new life, which are expressed in the social gospel.

Every forward step in the historical evolution of religion has been marked by a closer union of religion and ethics and by the elimination of non-ethical religious performances.   This union of religion and ethics reached its highest perfection in the life and mind of Jesus.   After him Christianity quickly dropped back to the pre-christian stage.   Ceremonial actions and orthodox beliefs became indispensable to salvation; they had a value of their own, quite apart from their bearing on conduct. Theology had the task of defending and inculcating these non-ethical ingredients of religion, and that pulled theology down.   It is clear that our Christianity is most Christian when religion and ethics are viewed as inseparable elements of the same single-minded and wholehearted life, in which the consciousness of God and the consciousness of humanity blend completely.   Any new movement in theology which emphatically asserts the union of religion and ethics is likely to be a wholesome and christianizing force in Christian thought. The social gospel is of that nature. It plainly concentrates religious interest on the great ethical problems of social life. It scorns the tithing of mint, anise and cummin, at which the Pharisees are still busy, and insists on getting down to the weightier matters of God's law, to justice and mercy. It ties up religion not only with duty, but with big duty that stirs the soul with religious feeling and throws it back on God for help. The non-ethical practices and beliefs in historical Christianity nearly all centre on the winning of heaven and immortality. On the other hand, the Kingdom of God can be established by nothing except righteous life and action. There is nothing in social Christianity which is likely to breed or reinforce superstition. The more the social gospel engages and inspires theological thought, the more will religion be concentrated on ethical righteousness. The social gospel is bound to be a reformatory and christianizing force inside of theology.

Theology is the esoteric thought of the Church. Some of its problems are unknown and unintelligible except where the Church keeps an interest in them alive. Even the terminology of theology is difficult for anyone to understand unless he has lived under church influence for years. Jesus and his followers were laymen. The people felt that his teaching was different from the arguments of their theologians, less ponderous and more moving. When Christianity worked its way from the lower to the higher classes, its social sympathies became less

democratic and fraternal, its language less simple, and
its ideas more speculative, elaborate and remote. Origen
felt he had to apologize for the homely Greek and the
simple arguments of Jesus. Theology became an affair
of experts. The first duty of the laymen was to believe
with all their hearts what they could not possibly understand with all their heads.

The practical result has been that laymen have always
assented as they were told, but have made an unconscious
private selection of the truths that seemed to contain
marrow for them. The working creed of the common
man is usually very brief. A man may tote a large load
of theology and live on a small part of it. If ministers
periodically examined their church members as professors examine their classes, they would find that a man
can be in the rain a long time and not become wetter
under the skin. Even in the Middle Ages, when all philosophy was theology and when religious doubt was rare,
the laity seem to have had their own system of faith. In
the memoirs of statesmen and artists and merchants, in
the songs of the common people, and in the secret sym-
bolism of the masons and other gilds, we find a simple
faith which guided their life. They believed in God and
his law, in immortality and retribution, in Christ and
his mercy, in the abiding difference between righteousness
and evil, and by this faith they tried to do their duty
where God had given them their job in life.

The social gospel approximates lay religion. It deals
with the ethical problems of the present life with which
the common man is familiar and which press upon his
conscience. Yet it appeals to God, his will, his kingdom;

to Christ, his spirit, his law. Audiences who are estranged from the Church and who would listen to theological terminology with frank scorn, will listen with absorbed interest to religious thought when it is linked with their own social problems.

Theology ought not to pare down its thought to the rudimentary ideas of untrained people. But every influence which compels it to simplify its terms and to deal with actual life is a blessing to theology. Theological professors used to lecture and write in Latin. There is perhaps no other language in which one can utter platitudes so sonorously and euphoniously. It must have been a sanitary sweating off of adipose tissue when theology began to talk in the vernacular. It will be a similar increase of health when theology takes in hand the problems of social redemption and considers how its doctrines connect with the Kingdom of God in actual realization.

The renovating effect of the social gospel would aid theology to meet the really modern religious needs. Heart religion is always a cry of need. Men pray because a burden is on their life; sickness threatens them; a child is in danger; some morbid passion has gained a footing in their mind or body and can not be shaken off; some evil has been done which can not be undone. The need is beyond their own strength. So they cry to a higher Power to help, to forgive, to cleanse, to save.

Now, many of the fears and burdens which drove men to the altars of their gods in the past are being eased in modern life. People are learning to trace diseases to natural causes instead of the evil eye, or the devil, or the anger of God. Even the streptococcus has a friendlier look than the omnipresent devils that haunt a Burmese hill tribe. Men used to feel acute guilt if they had committed some ritual oversight, such as touching a taboo thing, eating meat on Friday, or working on the Sabbath. The better teachings of modern Christianity and general religious indifference have combined to reduce that sort of fear and guilt.

On the other hand we are becoming much more sensitive about collective sins in which we are involved. I have a neighbour who owns stock in a New England cotton mill. Recently the company opened a factory in North Carolina and began to employ child labour. This man's young daughter faded away when she was emerging from childhood, and so he thinks of the other girls, who are breathing cotton fluff for him. A correspondent wrote me whose husband, a man of national reputation, had bought stock in a great steel company. She is a Jewess and a pacifist. When the plant began to devote itself to the manufacture of shrapnel and bombs in 1915, she felt involved. But what was her husband to do with the stock? Would it make things better if he passed the war-stained property to another man? I know a woman whose father, back in the nineties, took a fortune out of a certain dirty mill town. She is now living on his fortune; but the children of the mill-hands are living on their misfortune. No effort of hers can undo more than a fraction of the evil which was set in motion while that fortune was being accumulated.

If these burdens of conscience were foolish or morbid,

increased insight and a purer Christian teaching would lift them.   But it is increased insight and Christian feeling which created them.   An unawakened person does not inquire on whose life juices his big dividends are fattening.   Upper-class minds have been able to live parasitic lives without any fellow-feeling for the peasants or tenants whom they were draining to pay for their leisure.   Modern democracy brings these lower fellow-men up to our field of vision.   Then if a man has drawn any real religious feeling from Christ, his participation in the systematized oppression of civilization will, at least at times, seem an intolerable burden and guilt.   Is this morbid? Or is it morbid to live on without such realization? Those who to-day are still without a consciousness of collective wrong must be classified as men of darkened mind.

These are distinctly modern burdens.   They will continue to multiply and increase.   Does the old theology meet them?   Was it competent to meet the religious problems raised by the war?   Can personal forgiveness settle such accounts as some men run up with their fellowmen?   Does Calvinism deal adequately with a man who appears before the judgment seat of Christ with $50,000,-000 and its human corollaries to his credit, and then pleads a free pardon through faith in the atoning sacrifice?

Religious experience, as William James has shown us, has many varieties, and some are distinctly higher than others.   The form most common among us has come through an intense concentration on a man's own sins, his

needs, his destiny. In the Old Testament we have a
number of accounts describing how men of the highest
type of God-consciousness made their fundamental experience of God and received their prophetic mission. In
none of these cases did the prophet struggle for his personal salvation as later Christian saints have done. His
woe did not come through fear of personal damnation,
but through his sense of solidarity with his people and
through social feeling; his hope and comfort was not for
himself alone but for his nation. This form of religious
experience is more distinctively Christian than any form
which is caused by fear and which thinks only of self. It
contains larger possibilities of personal growth and religious power.

The social gospel creates a type of religious experience
corresponding closely to the prophetic type. It fuses the
Christian spirit and the social consciousness in a new out-
reaching toward God and in remarkable experiences of
his comfort and inspiring power. This is the most youthful, modern, and effective form of present-day religion.

Religious experience reacts on theology. Consider the
men who have turned theological thought into new channels — Paul, Augustine, Luther, Fox, Wesley, Schleiermacher. These were all men who had experienced God
at first hand and while under the pressure of new problems. Then they generalized on the basis of their experience. Paul, for instance, had borne the weight of
the Law; he had found his own efforts futile; he had
found Christ gracious, free, and a power of life. On this
experience he built his theology. A like experience under
Catholic legalism enabled Luther to understand Paul; he

revitalized the Pauline theology, built a theology of emancipation on that, and threw out of religious practice and thought what was not in agreement with his experience and its formula.

The rank and file of us have no genius and can not erect our personal experience into a common standard. But our early experiences act as a kind of guide by which we test what seems to have truth and reality. We select those theoretical ideas which agree with our experience, and are cold to those which have never entered into our life. When such a selective process is exercised by many active minds, who all act on the same lines, the total effect on theological thought is considerable. This is a kind of theological referendum, a democratic change in theology on the basis of religious experience.

Connect these two propositions: that an experience of religion through the medium of solidaristic social feeling is an experience of unusually high ethical quality, akin to that of the prophets of the Bible; and second, that a fresh and clearly marked religious experience reacts on theology. Can we not justly expect that the increasing influence of the social gospel and all that it stands for, will have a salutary influence on theology? The social gospel has already restored the doctrine of the Kingdom of God, which held first place with Jesus but which individualistic theology carefully wrapped in several napkins and forgot. Theology always needs rejuvenation. Most of all in a great epoch of change like ours. Yet change always hurts. If change must come, the influence of the social gospel is the most constructive and wholesome channel by which it could possibly come. Surely theology will not become less Christian by widening the scope of salvation, by taking more seriously the burden of social evil, and by learning to believe in the Kingdom of God. The proclamation of the social gospel would evoke the prophetic spirit in the exponents of doctrinal theology. Then they would have to seek boldness and authority from the living spirit of God. Theology has a right to the forward look and to the fire of religious vision.

CHAPTER III

NEITHER ALIEN NOR NOVEL

In these introductory chapters my aim is to win the benevolent and serious attention of conservative readers for the discussions that are to follow. I have thus far tried to show that the spread of the social gospel will inevitably react on theology, and that this influence is likely to be constructive and salutary. Let us add the important fact that the social gospel imports into theology nothing that is new or alien.

Frequent attempts have been made in the history of our religion to blend alien elements with it. The early Gnostics and the mediaeval Albigenses, for instance, tried to combine historical Christianity with dualistic conceptions of the universe and strict asceticism. Modern Mormonism, Theosophy, and Christian Science represent syncretistic formations, minglings of genuine Christianity with new and alien elements.

The belief in the universal reign of law, the doctrine of evolution, the control of nature by man, and the value of education and liberty as independent goods,— these are among the most influential convictions of modern life and have deeply modified our religious thought. But they are novel elements in theology. They are not alien, but certainly they held no such controlling position in the theology of the past as they do with us. We may dis-

cover prophetic forecasts of them in the Bible, but we
have to look for them.

On the other hand the idea of the redemption of the
social organism is nothing alien. It is simply a proper
part of the Christian faith in redemption from sin and
evil. As soon as the desire for salvation becomes strong
and intelligent enough to look beyond the personal sins
of the individual, and to discern how our personality in
its intake and output is connected with the social groups
to which we belong, the problem of social redemption is
before us and we can never again forget it. It lies like
a larger concentric circle around a smaller one. It is
related to our intimate personal salvation like astronomy
to physics. Only spiritual and intellectual immaturity
have kept us from seeing it clearly before. The social
gospel is not an alien element in theology.

Neither is it novel. The social gospel is, in fact, the
oldest gospel of all. It is " built on the foundation of the
apostles and prophets." Its substance is the Hebrew
faith which Jesus himself held. If the prophets ever
talked about the " plan of redemption," they meant the
social redemption of the nation. So long as John the
Baptist and Jesus were proclaiming the gospel, the Kingdom of God was its central word, and the ethical teaching of both, which was their practical commentary and
definition of the Kingdom idea, looked toward a higher
social order in which new ethical standards would become
practicable. To the first generation of disciples the hope
of the Lord's return meant the hope of a Christian social
order on earth under the personal rule of Jesus Christ,

and they would have been amazed if they had learned that
this hope was to be motioned out of theology and other
ideas substituted. The social gospel is nothing alien or novel. When it
comes to a question of pedigree and birth-right, it may
well turn on the dogmas on which the Catholic and Protestant theologies are based and inquire for their birth
certificate. They are neither dominant in the New Testament nor clearly defined in it. The more our historical
investigations are laying bare the roots of Catholic
dogma, the more do we see them running back into alien
Greek thought, and not into the substance of Christ's
message nor into the Hebrew faith. We shall not get
away again from the central proposition of Harnack's
History of Dogma, that the development of Catholic
dogma was the process of the Hellenization of Christianity; in other words, that alien influences streamed into the
religion of Jesus Christ and created a theology which he
never taught nor intended. What would Jesus have said
to the symbol of Chalcedon or the Athanasian Creed if
they had been read to him?

The doctrine of the Kingdom of God was left undeveloped by individualistic theology and finally mislaid by
it almost completely, because it did not support nor fit in
with that scheme of doctrine. In the older handbooks
of theology it is scarcely mentioned, except in the chapters
on eschatology; in none of them does it dominate the
table of contents. What a spectacle, that the original
teaching of our Lord has become an incongruous element
in so-called evangelical theology, like a stranger with
whom the other doctrines would not associate, and who

was finally ejected because he had no wedding garment! In the same way the distinctive ethics of Jesus, which is part and parcel of his Kingdom doctrine, was long the hidden treasure of suppressed democratic sects. Now, as soon as the social gospel began once more to be preached in our own time, the doctrine of the Kingdom was immediately loved and proclaimed afresh, and the ethical principles of Jesus are once more taught without reservation as the only alternative for the greedy ethics of capitalism and militarism. These antipathies and affinities are a strong proof that the social gospel is neither alien nor novel, but is a revival of the earliest doctrines of Christianity, of its radical ethical spirit, and of its revolutionary consciousness.

The body of ideas which we call the social gospel is not the product of a fad or temporary interest; it is not an alien importation or a novel invention; it is the revival of the most ancient and authentic gospel, and the scientific unfolding of essential elements of Christian doctrine which have remained undeveloped all too long; the rise of the social gospel is not a matter of choice but of destiny; the digestion of its ideas will exert a quickening and reconstructive influence on every part of theology.

The verification of these propositions lies in the future. But I believe that a survey of the history of theology during the last hundred years would already corroborate the inevitableness and the fruitfulness of the essential ideas of the social gospel. The trend of theology has been this way, and wherever the social nature of Christianity has been clearly understood, a new understanding for other theological problems has followed. The limits of this book do not permit such a survey, and I have not the accurate and technical knowledge of the literature of doctrinal theology to do justice to the subject. It would be an attractive subject for a specialist to trace the genesis and progress of the social gospel in systematic theology. The following paragraphs are simply by way of suggestion.

So far as my observation of doctrinal handbooks goes, it seems that those writers whose minds were formed before the eighties rarely show any clear comprehension of social points of view. We move in a different world of thought when we read their books. It would pay the reader to test this for himself by reading the table of contents and scanning crucial sections of any standard American theologian of the first half of the nineteenth century. The terms, the methods, the problems, and the guiding interests lie far away. If any social ideas do occur, they are most often the dutiful explanation of ideas derived from Hebrew religion. Those individuals of that era who did strike out into social conceptions of Christianity deserve the name and honour of prophets.

Among the earlier German theologians Friedrich Schleiermacher, Richard Rothe, and Albrecht Ritschl seem to me to deserve that title. The constructive genius of Schleiermacher worked out solidaristic conceptions of Christianity which were far ahead of his time. Ritschl built his essential ideas of the kingdom of evil and the Kingdom of God on Schleiermacher's work, and stressed the teaching of Luther that our service to God consists, not in religious performances, but in the faithful work we do in our secular calling. The practical importance of these elements of Ritschl's theology is proved by the strong social spirit pervading the younger Ritschlian school. The moderate liberals grouped in the "Evangelisch-soziale Kongress" and organized as "Freunde der Christlichen Welt" and "Freunde evangelischer Freiheit" all have social orientation. Professor Herrmann and Professor Troeltsch have definitely faced the relation between systematic theology and the social task of Christianity. The monumental work of Troeltsch, "die Soziallehren der christlichen Kirchen und Gruppen," is the first and chief attempt to apply the methods of the history of doctrine to the social convictions and hopes of the Churches. Conservative theology is naturally less responsive to the newer influences. But the wonderful work of the "Innere Mission" since Wichern, and the social reconstruction of Germany, in which the conservative parts of the nation have taken a full share, have not left their conception of the mission of Christianity untouched.

Switzerland democratizes whatever it handles. The "Religiös-sozialen" in German Switzerland have more political radicalism and more religious enthusiasm for the doctrine of the Kingdom of God than the corresponding German groups. They have done thorough and inspiring work on the combination of social and theological ideas, especially Ragaz, Kutter, Matthieu, Benz, and Reinhardt.

Social and democratic idealism is one of the most active ingredients in Catholic Modernism. The French Protestants, though they number only about 700,000, have produced a social and socialist literature of a richness and maturity which puts our greater numbers to shame, and witnesses to the intellectual fertility of French life. Auguste Sabatier, Charles Secrétan, Tomy Fallot, Wilfred Monod, Elie Gounelle, and Paul Passy occur to me among those who have given doctrinal formulation to the social gospel.

Great Britain has been the foremost capitalistic nation for a century and a half. Its religion and theology have necessarily matched its individualistic political economy and political philosophy. When the early Christian Socialists, Frederick Denison Maurice and Charles Kingsley, first asserted solidaristic ideas on theology and social questions, they justly felt that they were preaching a new and prophetic gospel in the midst of a Babylon of competitive selfishness. The trend of things is strikingly brought out by the contrast between their lonely position in the revolutionary year of 1848 and the Anglican Congress of 1908, where Christian Socialism was in possession of the platform and only Lord Cecil made a stand against it. It is significant that, so far as the social gospel is concerned, the High Church section has become Broad, and some of its intellectual leaders are weaving solidaristic ideas into their most sacramental and ecclesiastical doctrines. At the same time the Free Church leaders have worked their way out of individualistic Evangelicalism, and are freely applying their heritage of democratic faith to the social problems.

Of course I am not now discussing the popular propaganda of social Christianity, nor the growth of organizations for its practical application, but simply the reaction of the social gospel on doctrinal theology.[1] In our country, many of the younger men in the North who have written on theology have shown that the problems of society are a vital concern with them, and their fresh theological work consists largely in understanding the relation between social life and religion. I am thinking of William A. Brown, John W. Buckham, William H. P. Faunce, Thomas B. Hall, William DeWitt Hyde, Rufus Jones, Henry C. King, Shailer Mathews, Francis G. Peabody, Gerald B. Smith, George B. Stevens, and James B. Thomas, but I am sure this enumeration is very incomplete. Some of the best work is done in the class rooms, and has not yet come out in print.

When we contrast the neglect of the social contents of Christianity in former generations, and the fertile intellectual work now being given to this part of theology, a strong probability is established that the social gospel is not a passing interest, but that it is bound to become one of the permanent and commanding ingredients of theology.

[1] I sketched the Social Awakening in the Churches in the first part of "Christianizing the Social Order." But that was written in 1912.

CHAPTER IV

THE CONSCIOUSNESS OF SIN

It remains now to pass in review the doctrines which would be affected by the social gospel and which ought to give more adequate expression to it. On some of the more speculative doctrines the social gospel has no contribution to make. Its interests lie on earth, within the social relations of the life that now is. It is concerned with the eradication of sin and the fulfilment of the mission of redemption. The sections of theology which ought to express it effectively, therefore, are the doctrines of sin and redemption.

The Christian consciousness of sin is the basis of all doctrines about sin. A serious and humble sense of sinfulness is part of a religious view of life. Our consciousness of sin deepens as our moral insight matures and becomes religious. When we think on the level of law or public opinion, we speak of crime, vice, bad habits, or defective character. When our mind is in the attitude of religion, we pray: "Create in me a clean heart, O God, and renew a right spirit within me." When a man is within the presence and consciousness of God, he sees himself and his past actions and present conditions in the most searching light and in eternal connections. To lack the consciousness of sin is a symptom of moral immaturity or of an effort to keep the shutters down and the light out. The most highly developed individuals, who have the power of interpreting life for others, and who have the clearest realization of possible perfection and the keenest hunger for righteousness, also commonly have the most poignant sense of their own shortcomings.

By our very nature we are involved in tragedy. In childhood and youth we have imperious instincts and desires to drive us, and little knowledge to guide and control us. We commit acts of sensuality, cruelty, or dishonour, which nothing can wipe from our memory. A child is drawn into harmful habits which lay the foundation for later failings, and which may trip the man again when his powers begin to fail in later life. How many men and women have rushed with the starry eyes of hope into relations which brought them defilement of soul and the perversion of their most intimate life, but from which they could never again extricate themselves by any wrench. "Forgive us our trespasses. Lead us not into temptation." The weakness or the stubbornness of our will and the tempting situations of life combine to weave the tragic web of sin and failure of which we all make experience before we are through with our years.

Any religious tendency or school of theology must be tested by the question whether it does justice to the religious consciousness of sin. Now, one cause of distrust against the social gospel is that its exponents often fail to show an adequate appreciation of the power and guilt of sin. Its teachings seem to put the blame for wrongdoing on the environment, and instead of stiffening and awakening the sense of responsibility in the individual, it teaches him to unload it on society. There is doubtless truth in this accusation. The emphasis on environment and on the contributory guilt of the community, does offer a chance to unload responsibility, and human nature is quick to seize the chance. But the old theology has had its equivalents for environment. Men unloaded on original sin, on the devil, and on the decrees of God. Adam began soon after the fall to shift the blame. This shiftiness seems to be one of the clearest and most universal effects of original sin.

Moreover, there is an unavoidable element of moral unsettlement whenever the religious valuation of sin is being reconsidered. Paul frequently and anxiously defended his gospel against the charge that his principle of liberty invited lawlessness, and that under it a man might even sin the more in order to give grace the greater chance. We know what the Hebrew prophets thought of the sacrificial cult and moral righteousness, but we are not informed about the unsettling effect which their teaching may have had. If we could raise up some devout priest of the age of Amos or Isaiah to give us his judgment on the theology of the prophets, he would probably assure us that these men doubtless meant well, but that they had no adequate sense of sin; they belittled the sacrifices instituted by Moses; but sacrificing, as all men knew, was the true expression and gauge of repentance.

In the early years of the Reformation, Catholic observers noted a distressing looseness in the treatment of sin. Men no longer searched their consciences in the confessional; they performed no works of penance to render satisfaction to God and to prove their contrition; they no longer used the ascetic means of holiness to subdue their flesh and to gain victory over the powers of darkness. Luther had taught them that God required nothing but faith, and that all accounts could be squared by agreeing to call them square. By any standard of measurement known to Catholics, the profounder consciousness of sin was with the old theology and its practical applications. In point of fact, the Reformation did upset the old means of moral control and did create widespread demoralization. But in time, Geneva, Holland, or Scotland showed a deeper consciousness of sin than Rome or Paris. The sense of sin found new outlets.

The delinquencies of a new movement are keenly observed because they are new; the shortcomings of an old system are part of the accepted scheme of life. If the exponents of the old theology have taught humanity an adequate consciousness of sin, how is it that they themselves have been blind and dumb on the master iniquities of human history? During all the ages while they were the theological keepers of the conscience of Christendom, the peasants in the country and the working class in the cities were being sucked dry by the parasitic classes of society, and war was damning poor humanity. Yet what traces are there in traditional theology that the minds of old-line theologians were awake to these magnificent manifestations of the wickedness of the human heart? How is it that only in the modern era, since the moral insight of mankind has to some extent escaped from the tuition of the old theology, has a world-wide social movement arisen to put a stop to the exploitation of the poor, and that only in the last three years has war been realized as the supreme moral evil? One of the culminating accusations of Jesus against the theological teachers of his time was that they strained out gnats and swallowed camels, judiciously laying the emphasis on the minor sins and keeping silence on the profitable major wrongs. It is possible to hold the orthodox doctrine on the devil and not recognize him when we meet him in a real estate office or at the stock exchange.

A health officer of Toronto told me a story which illustrates the consciousness of sin created by the old religious teaching. If milk is found too dirty, the cans are emptied and marked with large red labels. This hits the farmer where he lives. He may not care about the health of Toronto, but he does care for the good opinion of his own neighbourhood, and when he drives to the station and finds his friends chuckling over the red labels on his cans, it acts as a moral irritant. One day a Mennonite farmer found his cans labeled and he swore a worldly oath. The Mennonites are a devout people who take the teachings of Christ seriously and refuse to swear, even in law-courts. This man was brought before his church and excluded. But, mark well, not for introducing cow-dung into the intestines of babies, but for expressing his belief in the damnation of the wicked in a non-theological way. When his church will hereafter have fully digested the social gospel, it may treat the case this way: "Our brother was angry and used the name of God profanely in his anger; we urge him to settle this alone with God. But he has also defiled the milk supply by unclean methods. Having the life and health of young children in his keeping, he has failed in his trust. Voted, that he be excluded until he has proved his lasting repentance." The result would be the same, but the sense of sin would do its work more intelligently.

In his " Appeal to the Christian Nobility," Luther said that in consequence of the many fast days and the insistence of the priests on their observance, the people had come to a point where they regarded it as a greater sin to eat butter on a fast day than to lie, swear, or commit fornication. An eminent minister in New York enumerated as the chief marks of a Christian that he attends church, reads the Bible, and contributes to the support of public worship. A less eminent minister in the same place mentioned as the four sins from which a Christian must abstain, drinking, dancing, card playing, and going to the movies. And this in New York where the capitalistic system of the nation comes to a head!

It may well be that with some individuals there is a loss of seriousness in the sense of sin as a result of the social gospel. But on the whole the result consists chiefly in shifting the emphasis and assigning a new valuation to different classes of sins. Attention is concentrated on questions of public morality, on wrongs done by whole classes or professions of men, on sins which enervate and submerge entire mill towns or agricultural states. These sins have been side-stepped by the old theology. We now have to make up for a fatal failure in past teaching.

We feel a deep consciousness of sin when we realize that we have wasted our years, dissipated our energies, left our opportunities unused, frustrated the grace of

God, and dwarfed and shamed the personality which God intended when he called us into life.   It is a similar and even deeper misery to realize that our past life has hurt and blocked the Kingdom of God, the sum of all good, the essential aim of God himself.   Our duty to the Kingdom of God is on a higher level than all other duties. To aid it is the supreme joy.   To have failed it by our weakness, to have hampered it by our ignorance, to have resisted its prophets, to have contradicted its truths, to have denied it in time of danger, to have betrayed it for thirty pieces of silver,— this is the most poignant consciousness of sin.   The social gospel opens our eyes to the ways in which religious men do all these things.   It plunges us in a new baptism of repentance.

CHAPTER V

THE FALL OF MAN

WE are familiar with the teachings of traditional theology on the first entrance of sin into the life of the race: the state of innocence of our first parents; the part played by Satan in tempting them; the motives and experiences of the fall; the apostasy of the entire race through the disobedience of its head; the transmission of depravity and death to all; the imputation of Adam's guilt to all his descendants; the ruin of the divine plan for humanity by the perversity of sin.

The motives of theology in elaborating so fully an event so remote were partly philosophical and partly religious.

The philosophical motive was the desire for a coherent explanation of our universe and its present baffling mixture of good and evil. The story of the fall, as interpreted by theology, furnished an outline for a philosophical history of the race. It was the first act in a great racial tragedy which was to end with the final judgment. The fact that a mind like Milton's took the fall as the theme for a great epic, and that his poem was accepted as a poetic treatment of the highest realities, shows how the doctrine of the fall dominated common thought.

The religious motive in elaborating the doctrine of the fall was the desire to bring all men under conviction of

sin and condemnation in order that all might realize their
need of grace and salvation. There was no need to prove
the guilt of any one individual when all were in a state
of corruption. It was not a question of this act or that,
but of the state of apostasy from which all acts proceeded
and by which even our virtues are contaminated. The
terribleness of sin became clear only by scanning the
height from which man had fallen. He once had a pure
consciousness of God; he now has a mind darkened by
sin and unable to know God. He had a will set on holiness; he now has a will set on evil and rebellion. He had
love of goodness, harmony of the higher and lower powers, freedom from suffering, power over nature, and the
grace of God. He lost it all. Consequently he is unable
to save himself. Only the grace of God can save him.
We can see this religious motive at work in the great theologians of sin and grace, Paul, Augustine, Luther, and
Calvin. They abased man to glorify God's mercy. They
took away all " boasting." They shut all doors on the
prisoner of sin except the door of grace in order to compel him to emerge through that.

It is important to realize that the story of the fall is incomparably more fundamental in later theology than it
was in biblical thought. The conspicuous place given to
Genesis in the arrangement of the Hebrew canon, itself
concentrated the attention of later times on it. The story
now embodied in Genesis iii was part of the Jahvist narrative, a document of Ephraimitic origin dating back to
the ninth century B.C. The original purpose of the story
was not to explain the origin of sin, but the origin of

death and evil. There are scarcely any allusions to the
story in the Old Testament. The prophets were deeply
conscious of the sins of men, but they did not base their
teachings on the doctrine of the fall. Not till we reach
post-biblical Jewish theology is there any general interest
in the story of Adam's fall. Even then the story of the
fall of the angels in Genesis vi attracted more interest.

In the synoptic sayings of Jesus there is not even a
reference to the fall of Adam. In the fourth gospel
there is one allusion, (John viii, 44). Jesus, of course,
had the clearest consciousness of the chasm between the
will of God and the actual condition of mankind. The
universality of sin was a matter of course with him; it was
presupposed in all his teaching. But he was concerned
only with those sources of sin which he saw in active work
about him: first, the evil heart of man from which all
evil words and actions proceed; second, the social stum-
bling blocks of temptation which make the weak to fall;
and third, the power of the Kingdom of Evil. On the
other hand the first origin of evil seems to have been
so distant in his mind that it did not readily slip into any
discussions of sin which are preserved to us. His interest was practical and not speculative, religious and ethical
and not philosophical.

Not until we come to Paul do we find any full and
serious use of the story of the fall in the Bible. He twice
(Romans v and I Corinthians xv) set over against each
other the carnal humanity descended from Adam and
characterized by sin and mortality, and the spiritual humanity descended from Christ and characterized by holiness and eternal life. These passages belong to the theo-

logical portions of Paul's writings and were eagerly
seized by the patristic writers as congenial raw material
for their work.

When once theology concentrated on the story it was
expanded by exegetical inferences, by allegorical embel-
lishments, and by typology, until it conveyed far more
than it actually contained. It comes as a shock to realize, for instance, that the story in Genesis itself does
not indicate that the writer understood the serpent to be
Satan, or Satan to be speaking through the serpent.
Moreover, we find so few traces of any belief in Satan
in Hebrew thought before the Exile that it seems doubt-
ful if contemporary readers would have understood him
to be meant unless further indications made the reference clear.

Here, then, we have two different methods of treating the story of the fall. Theology has given it basic
importance. It has built its entire scheme of thought
on the doctrine of the fall. Jesus and the prophets paid
little or no attention to it. They were able to see sin
clearly and to fight it with the highest energy without
depending on the doctrine of the fall for a footing.
Only with Paul is the story clearly of religious importance, and even with him it is not as central as for instance the antagonism between spirit and flesh. It offered him a wide spiritual perspective and a means of
glorifying Christ.

Two things seem to follow. First, that the traditional doctrine of the fall is the product of speculative
interest mainly, and that the most energetic consciousness of sin can exist without drawing strength from this

doctrine. Second, that if the substance of Scriptural thought, the constant and integral trend of biblical convictions, is the authoritative element in the Bible, the doctrine of the fall does not seem to have as great an authority as it has long exercised.

How does this affect the special gospel? What doctrinal teaching on this point is able to give it the most effective backing?

The social gospel is above all things practical. It needs religious ideas which will release energy for heroic opposition against organized evil and for the building of a righteous social life. It would find entire satisfaction in the attitude of Jesus and the prophets who dealt with sin as a present force and did not find it necessary to indoctrinate men on its first origin. It would have no motive to be interested in a doctrine which diverts attention from the active factors of sin which can be influenced, and concentrates attention on a past event which no effort of ours can influence.

Theology has made the catastrophe of the fall so complete that any later addition to the inheritance of sin seems slight and negligible. What can be worse than a state of total depravity and active enmity against God and his will? [1] Consequently theology has had little to say about the contributions which our more recent fore-

[1] The Helvetic Confession, II, Chapter 8: "We understand original sin to be the native corruption of man which has passed from our first parents to us; through which, being sunk in depraved desires, averse to good, inclined to every evil, full of every wickedness, of contempt and hatred of God, we are unable to do or even to think any good whatever."

fathers have made to the sin and misery of mankind. The social gospel would rather reserve some blame for them, for their vices have afflicted us with syphilis, their graft and their wars have loaded us with public debts, and their piety has perpetuated despotic churches and unbelievable creeds. One of the greatest tasks in religious education reserved for the social gospel is to spread in society a sense of the solidarity of successive generations and a sense of responsibility for those who are to come after us and whom we are now outfitting with the fundamental conditions of existence. This is one of the sincerest and most durable means of spiritual restraint. It is hard to see how the thought of Adam and Eve can very directly influence young men and women who are to be the ancestors of new generations. In so far as the doctrine of the fall has made all later actions of negligible importance by contrast, it blocks the way for an important advance in the consciousness of sin.

The traditional doctrine of the fall has taught us to regard evil as a kind of unvarying racial endowment, which is active in every new life and which can be overcome only by the grace offered in the Gospel and ministered by the Church. It would strengthen the appeal of the social gospel if evil could be regarded instead as a variable factor in the life of humanity, which it is our duty to diminish for every young life and for every new generation.

These, it seems to me, are the points at which the social gospel impinges on the doctrine of the fall of man.

Of course evolutionary thought has radically changed the conceptions about the origin of the race for those whose thinking is done under the influence of evolutionary science. Such will take little interest in the discussion of this chapter. But there are many conservative minds who can not recast their thought in wholly new moulds; the story of the fall is a serious religious and intellectual burden to some of them. The more theology bases all its reasoning on the doctrine of the fall, the greater is the collapse and mental distress when a man comes to realize that the biblical story of the fall will not bear the tremendous weight which the theological system of the past has put upon it. For such the attitude suggested in this chapter seems to offer a way which is satisfying to both the religious and the scientific conscience. They can not be going far wrong if they take the attitude taken by the Hebrew prophets and by Jesus himself, concentrating their energies on the present and active sources of evil and leaving the question of the first origin of evil to God. On that basis it is possible to preach both an individualistic and a social gospel with full effectiveness.

CHAPTER VI

THE NATURE OF SIN

IT is not easy to define sin, for sin is as elastic and complicated as life itself. Its quality, degree, and culpability vary according to the moral intelligence and maturity of the individual, according to his social freedom, and his power over others. Theologians have erred, it seems to me, by fitting their definitions to the most highly developed forms of sin and then spreading them over germinal and semi-sinful actions and conditions.

We are equipped with powerful appetites. We are often placed in difficult situations, which constitute overwhelming temptations. We are all relatively ignorant, and while we experiment with life, we go astray. Some of our instincts may become rampant and overgrown, and then trample on our inward freedom. We are gifted with high ideals, with a wonderful range of possibilities, with aspiration and longing, and also weighted with inertia and moral incapacity to achieve. We are keenly alive to the call of the senses and the pleasures of the moment, and only dimly and occasionally conscious of our own higher destiny, of the mystic value of personality in others, and of God.

This sensual equipment, this ignorance and inertia, out of which our moral delinquencies sprout, are part

45

of our human nature. We did not order it so. Instead
of increasing our guilt, our make-up seems to entitle us
to the forbearing judgment of every onlooker, especially
God. Yet no doubt we are involved in objective wrong
and evil; we frustrate our possibilities; we injure others;
we disturb the divine harmonies. We are unfree, unhappy, conscious of a burden which we are unable to lift
or escape.

Sin becomes guilt in the full sense in the degree in
which intelligence and will enter. We have the impulse
to live our life, to exercise our freedom, to express and
satisfy the limitless cravings in us, and we are impatient
of restraint. We know that our idleness or sensuality
will cripple our higher self, yet we want what we want.
We set our desires against the rights of others, and disregard the claims of mercy, of gratitude, or of parental
love. Our self-love is wrought up to hot ill-will, hate,
lying, slander, and malevolence. Men press their covetousness to the injury of society. They are willing to
frustrate the cause of liberty and social justice in whole
nations in order to hold their selfish social and economic
privileges. Men who were powerful enough to do so,
have left broad trails of destruction and enslavement
through history in order to satisfy their selfish caprice,
avarice, and thirst for glory.

Two things strike us as we thus consider the development of sin from its cotyledon leaves to its blossom and
fruit. First, that the element of selfishness emerges as
the character of sin matures. Second, that in the higher
forms of sin it assumes the aspect of a conflict between
the selfish Ego and the common good of humanity; or,

expressing it in religious terms, it becomes a conflict between self and God.

The three forms of sin,— sensuousness, selfishness, and godlessness,— are ascending and expanding stages, in which we sin against our higher self, against the good of men, and against the universal good.

Theology with remarkable unanimity has discerned that sin is essentially selfishness. This is an ethical and social definition, and is proof of the unquenchable social spirit of Christianity. It is more essentially Christian than the dualistic conception of the Greek Fathers, who thought of sin as fundamentally sensuousness and materiality, and saw the chief consequence of the fall in the present reign of death rather than in the reign of selfishness.

The definition of sin as selfishness furnishes an excellent theological basis for a social conception of sin and salvation. But the social gospel can contribute a good deal to socialize and vitalize it.

Theology pictures the self-affirmation of the sinner as a sort of solitary duel of the will between him and God. We get a mental image of God sitting on his throne in glory, holy and benevolent, and the sinner down below, sullenly shaking his fist at God while he repudiates the divine will and chooses his own. Now, in actual life such titanic rebellion against the Almighty is rare. Perhaps our Puritan forefathers knew more cases than we because their theological God was accustomed to issue arbitrary decrees which invited rebellion. We do not rebel; we dodge and evade. We kneel in lowly submission and kick our duty under the bed while God is not looking.

The theological definitions of sin have too much the flavour of the monarchical institutions under the spiritual influence of which they were first formed. In an absolute monarchy the first duty is to bow to the royal will. A man may spear peasants or outrage their wives, but crossing the king is another matter. When theological definitions speak of rebellion against God as the common characteristic of all sin, it reminds one of the readiness of despotic governments to treat every offence as treason. Sin is not a private transaction between the sinner and God. Humanity always crowds the audience-room when God holds court. We must democratize the conception of God; then the definition of sin will become more realistic.

We love and serve God when we love and serve our fellows, whom he loves and in whom he lives. We rebel against God and repudiate his will when we set our profit and ambition above the welfare of our fellows and above the Kingdom of God which binds them together.

We rarely sin against God alone. The decalogue gives a simple illustration of this. Theology used to distinguish between the first and second table of the decalogue; the first enumerated the sins against God and the second the sins against men. Jesus took the Sabbath commandment off the first table and added it to the second; he said the Sabbath is not a taboo day of God, but an institution for the good of man. The command to honour our parents is also ethical. There remain the first three commandments, against polytheism, image worship, and the misuse of the holy name. The worship of various gods and the use of idols is no longer one of our dangers. The misuse of the holy name has lost much of its religious significance since sorcery and magic have moved to the back-streets. On the other hand, the commandments of the second table grow more important all the time. Science supplies the means of killing, finance the methods of stealing, the newspapers have learned how to bear false witness artistically to a globeful of people daily, and covetousness is the moral basis of our civilization.

[God is not only the spiritual representative of humanity; he is identified with it. In him we live and move and have our being. In us he lives and moves, though his being transcends ours. He is the life and light in every man and the mystic bond that unites us all. He is the spiritual power behind and beneath all our aspirations and achievements. He works through humanity to realize his purposes, and our sins block and destroy the Reign of God in which he might fully reveal and realize himself. Therefore our sins against the least of our fellow-men in the last resort concern God. Therefore when we retard the progress of mankind, we retard the revelation of the glory of God. Our universe is not a despotic monarchy, with God above the starry canopy and ourselves down here; it is a spiritual commonwealth with God in the midst of us.

We are on Christian ground when we insist on putting humanity into the picture. Jesus always deliberately and energetically bound man and God together.

He would not let us deal with man apart from God, nor
with God apart from man. We can not have forgiveness from God while we refuse forgiveness to any man.
"What ye have done to these, ye have done to me; what
ye have not done to these, ye have not done to me."
This identification of the interests of God and man is
characteristic of the religion of Jesus. Wherever God
is isolated, we drop back to a pre-Christian stage of
religion.

Sin is essentially selfishness. That definition is more
in harmony with the social gospel than with any individualistic type of religion. The sinful mind, then, is
the unsocial and anti-social mind. To find the climax
of sin we must not linger over a man who swears, or
sneers at religion, or denies the mystery of the trinity,
but put our hands on social groups who have turned the
patrimony of a nation into the private property of a
small class, or have left the peasant labourers cowed,
degraded, demoralized, and without rights in the land.[1]
When we find such in history, or in present-day life,
we shall know we have struck real rebellion against God
on the higher levels of sin.

We have defined sin. But we need more than definition. We need realization of its nature in order to
secure the right religious attitude toward it.

Sin is always revealed by contrast to righteousness.
We get an adequate intellectual measure of it and feel

[1] I have just been reading "The Secret of Rural Depopulation,"
an account of the condition of the agricultural laborers in England,
by Lieut-Col. D. C. Pedder, 1904. Fabian Tract No. 118. The
Fabian Society, 3 Clement's Inn, Strand, W. C., London.

the proper hate and repugnance for it only when we see
it as the terrible defeat and frustration of a great good
which we love and desire.

Theology has tried to give us such a realization of
sin by elaborating the contrast between the sinless condition of Adam before the fall and his sinful condition
after it. But there are objections to this. In the first
place of course we do not know whether Adam was as
perfect as he is portrayed. Theology has ante-dated
conceptions of human perfection which we have derived
from Jesus Christ and has converted Adam into a perfect Christian. Paul does nothing of the kind. In the
second place, any interpretation of the nature of sin
taken from Adam will be imperfect, because Adam's
situation gave very limited opportunities for selfishness,
which is the essence of sin. He had no scope to exhibit
either the virtues or the sinful vices which come out in
the pursuits of commerce or politics. The only persons
with whom he could associate were God, Eve, and Satan.
Consequently theology lacked all social details in describing his condition before and after the fall. It could
only ascribe to him the virtues of knowing and loving
God and of having no carnal concupiscence, and, by
contrast, after the fall he lost the love and knowledge of
God and acquired carnal desires. Thus a fatal turn
toward an individualistic conception of sin was given to
theology through the solitariness of Adam.

A better and more Christian method of getting a religious realization of sin is to bring before our minds
the positive ideals of social righteousness contained in
the person of Christ and in the Kingdom of God, and

see sin as the treasonable force which frustrates and wrecks these ideals and despoils the earth of their enjoyment. It is Christ who convicts the world of sin and not Adam. The spiritual perfection of Jesus consists in the fact that he was so simply and completely filled with the love of God and man that he gave himself to the task of the Kingdom of God without any reservation or backsliding. This is the true standard of holiness. The fact that a man is too respectable to get drunk or to swear is no proof of his righteousness. His moral and religious quality must be measured by the intelligence and single-heartedness with which he merges his will and life in the divine purpose of the Kingdom of God. By contrast, a man's sinfulness stands out in its true proportion, not when he is tripped up by ill-temper or side-steps into shame, but when he seeks to establish a private kingdom of self-service and is ready to thwart and defeat the progress of mankind toward peace, toward justice, or toward a fraternal organization of economic life, because that would diminish his political privileges, his unearned income, and his power over the working classes.

It follows that a clear realization of the nature of sin depends on a clear vision of the Kingdom of God. We can not properly feel and know the reign of organized wrong now prevailing unless we constantly see it over against the reign of organized righteousness. Where the religious conception of the Kingdom of God is wanting, men will be untrained and unfit to see or to estimate the social manifestations of sin.

This proposition gives a solemn and terrible importance to the fact that doctrinal theology has failed to cherish and conserve for humanity the doctrine of the Kingdom of God. Christ died for it. Theology has allowed it to lead a decrepit, bed-ridden and senile existence in that museum of antiquities which we call eschatology. Having lost its vision of organized righteousness, theology necessarily lost its comprehension of organized sin, and therewith its right and power to act as the teacher of mankind on that subject. It saw private sin, and it set men to wrestling with their private doubts or sexual emotions by ascetic methods. But if sin is selfishness, how did that meet the case?

It would be unfair to blame theology for the fact that our race is still submerged under despotic government, under war and militarism, under landlordism, and under predatory industry and finance. But we can justly blame it for the fact that the Christian Church even now has hardly any realization that these things are large-scale sins. We can blame it in part for the fact that when a Christian minister in our country speaks of these sins he is charged with forgetting the simple gospel of sin and salvation, and is in danger of losing his position. This comes of shelving the doctrine of the Kingdom of God, or juggling feeble substitutes into its place. Theology has not been a faithful steward of the truth entrusted to it. The social gospel is its accusing conscience.

This is the chief significance of the social gospel for the doctrine of sin: it revives the vision of the Kingdom of God. When men see the actual world over against

the religious ideal, they become conscious of its constitutional defects and wrongs. Those who do their
thinking in the light of the Kingdom of God make less
of heresy and private sins. They reserve their shudders
for men who keep the liquor and vice trade alive against
public intelligence and law; for interests that organize
powerful lobbies to defeat tenement or factory legislation, or turn factory inspection into sham; for nations
that are willing to set the world at war in order to win
or protect colonial areas of trade or usurious profit from
loans to weaker peoples; and for private interests which
are willing to push a peaceful nation into war because
the stock exchange has a panic at the rumour of peace.
These seem the unforgivable sins, the great demonstrations of rebellious selfishness, wherever the social gospel
has revived the faith of the Kingdom of God.

Two aspects of the Kingdom of God demand special
consideration in this connection: the Kingdom is the
realm of love, and it is the commonwealth of labour.

Jesus Christ superimposed his own personality on the
previous conception of God and made love the distinctive characteristic of God and the supreme law of human
conduct. Consequently the reign of God would be the
reign of love. It is not enough to think of the Kingdom
as a prevalence of good will. The institutions of life
must be fundamentally fraternal and co-operative if
they are to train men to love their fellowmen as co-
workers. Sin, being selfish, is covetous and grasping.
It favours institutions and laws which permit unrestricted
exploitation and accumulation. This in turn sets up

antagonistic interests, increases law suits, class hostility, and wars, and so miseducates mankind that love and co-operation seem unworkable, and men are taught to put their trust in coercive control by the strong and in the sting of hunger and compulsion for the poor.

Being the realm of love, the Kingdom of God must also be the commonwealth of co-operative labour, for how can we actively love others without serving their *Marx?* needs by our abilities? If the Kingdom of God is a community of highly developed personalities, it must also be an organization for labour, for none can realize himself fully without labour. A divinely ordered community, therefore, would offer to all the opportunities of education and enjoyment, and expect from all their contribution of labour.

Here again we realize the nature of sin over against the religious ideal of society. Sin selfishly takes from others their opportunities for self-realization in order to increase its own opportunities abnormally; and it shirks its own labour and thereby abnormally increases the labour of others. Idleness is active selfishness; it is *Weber* not only unethical, but a sin against the Kingdom of God. *P.E.?* To lay a heavy burden of support on our fellows, usually on the weakest classes, and to do no productive labour in return, is so crude a manifestation of sinful selfishness that one would suppose only an occasional instance of such delinquency could be found, and only under medical treatment. But in fact throughout history the policy of most States has been shaped in order to make such a sinful condition easy and perpetual. Men who have been under the teachings of Christianity all their lives do not even see that parasitism is a sin. So deeply has our insight into sin been darkened by the lack of a religious ideal of social life. Henry Drummond, who was one of the early prophets of the Kingdom idea, long ago pointed out that parasites are on the way to perdition, physically, intellectually, and morally. We shall not be doing our thinking in a Christian way until we agree that productive labour according to the ability of each is one of " the conditions of salvation."

The accepted definition of sin as selfishness is therefore wholly in line with the social gospel, and the latter can back up the old theology with impressive examples of high-power selfishness which seem to have been overlooked. They can hardly fail to create a more searching consciousness of sin in every Christian mind. Indeed, many a Christian man, surveying the chief ambitions and results of his life in the light of the Kingdom of God, will have to begin his repentance over again and cry, *Mea culpa*.

There is evangelistic force in this social comprehension of the nature of sin. It offers searching and unsettling arguments and appeals to evangelistic preachers. If popular evangelists have not used them it can hardly be for lack of effectiveness. Is it because they are too effective?

If theology absorbs this understanding of the nature of sin, it will become a strong intellectual support of the social gospel, and come into fuller harmony with the spirit of the prophets and of the teaching of Jesus. The social gospel is part of the " return to Christ."

CHAPTER VII

THE TRANSMISSION OF SIN

How is sin transmitted from generation to generation? How is it made enduring and universal throughout the race?

This is by no means an academic question. Theology ought to be the science of redemption and offer scientific methods for the eradication of sin. In dealing with any epidemic disease, the first thing is to isolate the bacillus, and the second to see how it propagates and spreads. We must inquire for the lines of communication and contagion by which sin runs vertically down through history, and horizontally through the strata of contemporary society.

Theology has dealt with this problem in the doctrine of original sin. Many modern theologians are ready to abandon this doctrine, and among laymen it seems to carry so little sense of reality that audiences often smile at its mention. I take pleasure, therefore, in defending it. It is one of the few attempts of individualistic theology to get a solidaristic view of its field of work. This doctrine views the race as a great unity, descended from a single head, and knit together through all ages by unity of origin and blood. This natural unity is the basis and carrier for the transmission and universality of sin. Depravity of will and corruption of nature are transmitted wherever life itself is transmitted.

Science, to some extent, corroborates the doctrine of original sin. Evil does flow down the generations through the channels of biological coherence. Idiocy and feeble-mindedness, neurotic disturbances, weakness of inhibition, perverse desires, stubbornness and anti-social impulses in children must have had their adequate biological causes somewhere back on the line, even if we lack the records.

Even in normal individuals the animal instincts preponderate over the spiritual motives and restraints. All who have to train the young find themselves marshalling motives and forces to strengthen the higher desires against the drag of unwillingness. "The spirit is willing, but the flesh is weak," is a formula of Jesus. Paul's description of the struggle of flesh and spirit in his life is a classical expression of the tragedies enacted in the intimate life of every one who has tried to make his recalcitrant Ego climb the steep path of perfection: "The good which I would I do not; but the evil which I would not, that I practise."

According to orthodox theology man's nature passed through a fatal debasement at the beginning of history. According to evolutionary science the impulses connected with our alimentary and reproductive organs run far back in the evolution of the race and are well established and imperious, whereas the social, altruistic, and spiritual impulses are of recent development and relatively weak.

We can take our choice of the explanations. In either case a faulty equipment has come down to us through the reproductive life of the race.

There is, then, a substance of truth in this unpopular doctrine of original sin. But the old theology overworked it. It tried to involve us in the guilt of Adam as well as in his debasement of nature and his punishment of death. It fixed on us all a uniform corruption, and made it so complete that all evil resulting from personal sins seems trivial and irrelevant. If our will is so completely depraved, where do we get the freedom on which alone responsibility can be based? If a child is by nature set on evil, hostile to God, and a child of the devil, what is the use of education? For education presupposes an appetite for good which only needs awakening, direction, and spiritual support.

The texts usually cited in support of the doctrine can not justly be made to bear such universal significance.[1] The proof-text method, in trying to prove our original sin, has proved its own. The basic passage in Romans v, 12–21, is so difficult that even the exact methods of modern exegesis have not made Paul's meaning sure. Augustine based his influential argument on the Vulgate translation of verse 12, which is certainly faulty.

Theology was right in emphasizing the biological transmission of evil on the basis of race solidarity, but it strained the back of the doctrine by overloading it. On the other hand, it slighted or overlooked the fact

[1] Gen. vi, 5 : viii, 21 : Psalms xiv, 1–3: li, 5; lviii, 3; Isaiah xlviii, 8; John iii, 5–6; Romans v, 12–14; Eph. ii, 3.

that sin is transmitted along the lines of social tradition. This channel is at least as important as the other and far more susceptible of religious influence and control. Original sin deals with dumb forces of nature; social tradition is ethical and may be affected by conscious social action. Only the lack of social information and orientation in the past can explain the fact that theology has made so little of this.

The evil habits of boyhood,— lying, stealing, cigarette smoking, profane and obscene talk, self-pollution,— are usually set up in boys by the example and social suasion of boys just one stage older than they, young enough to be trusted companions, and old enough to exercise authority. One generation corrupts the next.

The permanent vices and crimes of adults are not transmitted by heredity, but by being socialized; for instance, alcoholism and all drug evils; cruel sports, such as bull-fights and pugilism; various forms of sex perversity; voluntary deformities, such as foot-binding, corseting, piercing of ears and nose; blood-feuds in Corsica; lynching in America. Just as syphilitic corruption is forced on the helpless fœtus in its mother's womb, so these hereditary social evils are forced on the individual embedded in the womb of society and drawing his ideas, moral standards, and spiritual ideals from the general life of the social body.

That sin is lodged in social customs and institutions and is absorbed by the individual from his social group is so plain that any person with common sense can observe it, but I have found only a few, even among the modern hand-books of theology, which show a clear recognition of the theological importance of this fact.[1] The social gospel has from the first emphasized it, and our entire religious method of dealing with children, adolescents, students, industrial and professional groups, and neighbourhoods, is being put on a different basis in consequence of this new insight. Systematic theology is not running even with practical theology at this point. A theology for the social gospel would have to say that original sin is partly social. It runs down the generations not only by biological propagation but also by social assimilation.

Theologians sometimes dispatch this matter easily as "the force of evil example." There is much more in it. We deal here not only with the instinct of imitation, but with the spiritual authority of society over its members.

In the main the individual takes over his moral judgments and valuations from his social class, profession, neighbourhood, and nation, making only slight personal modifications in the group standards. Only earnest or irresponsible persons are likely to enter into any serious

[1] O. Kirn, "Grundriss der evangelischen Dogmatik," p. 82: "Heredity is not the only channel through which sin is spread and increased. Defective education, evil example, and the direct incitement to sin by unjust treatment or seduction, are of at least equal importance. The sin that we inherit is only a fragment of the totality of sin existing in the race. We ought especially to replace the theological conception of hereditary guilt by the realization of the fact that guilt attaches not only to the individual, but that there is a common guilt of social groups in widening circles, till we reach the guilt of the whole race for the moral conditions pervading all humanity." See also Clarke, "Outline of Christian Theology," pp. 218–221; Brown, "Christian Theology in Outline," p. 278; Pfleiderer, "Grundriss der christlichen Glaubens-und Sittenlehre," p. 122.

opposition or contradiction, and then often on a single matter only, which exhausts their power of opposition. The deep marks which such a struggle with our group, especially in youth, leaves on our memory shows how hard it was at the time.

A group may be better or worse than a given member in it. It may require more neatness, fortitude, efficiency, and hard work than he is accustomed to. In that case the boy entering a good shop or a fine college fraternity is very promptly educated upward. On the other hand, if a group practises evil, it will excuse or idealize it, and resent any private judgment which condemns it. Evil then becomes part of the standards of morality sanctioned by the authority of society. This confuses the moral judgment of the individual. The faculty of inhibition goes wrong. The magnetic pole itself shifts and the compass-needle of conscience swings to S.E.

Theology has always been deeply interested in the problem of authority in religion. The problem of authority in sin is of equal importance. Religious faith in the individual would be weak and intermittent unless it could lean on permanent social authorities. Sin in the individual is shame-faced and cowardly except where society backs and protects it. This makes a decisive difference in the practical task of overcoming a given evil.

The case of alcoholic intoxication may serve as an example. Intoxication, like profanity and tattooing, is one of the universal marks of barbarism. In civilization it is a survival, and its phenomena become increasingly intolerable and disgusting to the scientific and to the moral mind. Nevertheless alcoholic drinking customs have prevailed and still prevail throughout civilization. What has given the practice of injecting a seductive drug into the human organism so enduring a hold? Other drug habits, such as the opium, cocaine, or heroin habits, are secretive and ashamed. Why does the alcohol habit flourish in the open? Aside from the question of the economic forces behind it, of which I shall speak later, the difference is due to social authority.

In the wine-drinking countries wine is praised in poetry and song. The most charming social usages are connected with its use. It is the chief reliance for entertainment and pleasure. Laughter is supposed to die without it. No disgrace is attached to mild intoxication provided a gentleman carries his drink well and continues to behave politely. Families take more pride in their wine-cellars than in the tombs of their ancestors. Young men are proud of the amount of wine and beer they can imbibe and of the learning which they refuse to imbibe. Until very recent years a total abstainer in middle class European society was regarded with disquietude of mind and social impatience, like a person advocating force revolution or political assassination. He was a heretic, and his freedom of conscience had to be won by very real sufferings.

This justification and idealization of alcoholism by public opinion made it incomparably harder to save the victims, to prevent the formation of the drinking habits in new cases, and to secure legislation. Governments were, of course, anxious to suppress the disgusting drunkenness of the labouring classes, which interfered with their working efficiency, but the taming of the liquor trade was hard to secure as long as men high up in Parliament, the established Church, and Society considered investments in breweries, distilleries, and public houses a perfectly honourable source of income. The rapid progress in the expulsion of the liquor trade in America would have been impossible if the idealization of the drinking customs had not previously disappeared from public opinion. The chief plea of the brewers now is that beer displaces distilled liquor and promotes temperance. In "the People's Sunday Evening," a popular theatre meeting in Rochester, N. Y., we have for seven years publicly invited and challenged the Brewers' Exchange and all the liquor trade organizations to discuss the social and moral utility of moderate drinking on our platform. They accepted the first time, but had to go to Buffalo for a lawyer to make the speech. After that we were never able to secure a response. The use of liquor is still common in America, but its social authority has been overcome. So far as I can see, this was done by the churches before either business or science lent much aid, and the decisive fact which set the voice of some of the denominations free was their refusal to tolerate in their membership persons financially interested in the liquor business, or to receive contributions from them.

In the case of alcoholism we can watch a gradual breaking down of the social authority of a great evil. In the case of militarism we are watching the reverse process. Before the War the military institutions of our nation were weak and public opinion condemned war. Enthusiasm for peace was one of the clearest social convictions of the Church. This state of mind was one of the causes for our mental reactions at the outbreak of the war. In the course of three years we have swung around. At first preparedness was advocated as a dire necessity under the actual circumstances. But soon other voices began to mingle with this. We were soft and flabby, without training in order and obedience. It would do our boys and young men a world of good to be under military discipline and drill for years. It would improve the American character. Prophets of war asserted that war is essentially noble, the supreme test of manhood and of the worth of a nation. The corresponding swing in the attitude of the churches was made slowly and with deep reluctance and searching of heart by many ministers. But it was made. Those who remained faithful to the religious peace convictions which had been orthodox a short time ago, were now extremists, and the position of a public spokesman of religion became exceedingly difficult for one who believed that war is inherently evil and in contradiction to Christianity. The problem of Jesus took on new forms and dealt with his pacifism and non-resistance. The ejection of the traders from the temple with a scourge of small cords, and the advice to the disciples to sell their cloaks and buy swords, took rank as important parts of the gospel.

In these ways religion, being part of the national life, had to adjust its convictions and teachings in order to permit the idealization of war. If the nations emerge into a long peace with disarmament, this war will be recorded as a holy and redemptive war. If preparedness and universal service become permanent institutions of American life, profound changes in the popular philosophy of life and in religious thought will follow. Social institutions always generate the theories adapted to them.

The idealization of evil is an indispensable means for its perpetuation and transmission. But the most potent motive for its protection is its profitableness. Ordinarily sin is an act of weakness and side-stepping, followed by shame the next day. But when it is the source of prolific income, it is no longer a shame-faced vagabond slinking through the dark, but an army with banners, entrenched and defiant. The bigger the dividends, the stiffer the resistance against anything that would cut them down. When fed with money, sin grows wings and claws.

The other outlets for sinful selfishness, such as overeating and sexual excess, soon reach their natural limit and end in nausea and disgust, or they eliminate the sinner. Polygamy gave full scope to the lust of great men, but Solomon's thousand concubines seem to be the limit in history and story. We have never heard of a man becoming a millionaire in the line of wives.

Property, too, used to be limited. Too much land or cattle or clothing became unmanageable. The main satisfaction of the rich was to have many guests and dependents, and to spend bountifully. The rise of the money system enlarged the limits of acquisition. Money could be bred from money. To-day a man can store millions in paper evidences of wealth in a safe deposit box, and collect the income from it with a stenographer,

a lawyer, and a pair of shears.   He can acquire tens of
millions, hundreds of millions.   Imagine the digestive
organs expanding to the size of a Zeppelin.

If "the love of money is the root of all evil," and if
selfishness is the essence of sin, such an expansion of the
range and storage capacity of selfishness must necessarily mark a new era in the history of sin, just as the
invention of the steam-engine marked a new era in the
production of wealth.   Drink, over-eating, sexualism,
vanity, and idleness are still reliable standardized sins.
But the exponent of gigantic evil on the upper ranges
of sin, is the love of money and the love of power over
men which property connotes.   This is the most difficult
field of practical redemption and the most necessitous
chance of evangelism.

The theological doctrine of original sin is an important effort to see sin in its totality and to explain its unbroken transmission and perpetuation.   But this explanation of the facts is very fragmentary, and theology
has done considerable harm in concentrating the attention of religious minds on the biological transmission of
evil.   It has diverted our minds from the power of
social transmission, from the authority of the social
group in justifying, urging, and idealizing wrong, and
from the decisive influence of economic profit in the de-
fense and propagation of evil.   These are ethical facts,
but they have the greatest religious importance, and they
have just as much right to being discussed in theology
as the physical propagation of the species, or creationism
and traducianism.   There is the more inducement to

teach clearly on the social transmission and perpetuation of sin because the ethical and religious forces can really do something to check and prevent the transmission of sin along social channels, whereas the biological transmission of original sin, except for the possible influence of eugenics, seems to be beyond our influence.

CHAPTER VIII

THE SUPER-PERSONAL FORCES OF EVIL

INDIVIDUALISTIC theology has not trained the spiritual intelligence of Christian men and women to recognize and observe spiritual entities beyond the individual. Our religious interest has been so focused on the soul of the individual and its struggles that we have remained uneducated as to the more complex units of spiritual life.

The chief exception to this statement is our religious insight into the history of Israel and Judah, into the nature of the family, and the qualities of the Church. The first of these we owe to the solidaristic vision of the Old Testament prophets who saw their nation as a gigantic personality which sinned, suffered, and repented. The second we owe to the deep interest which the Church from the beginning has taken in the purity of family life and the Christian nurture of the young. The third we owe to the high valuation the Church has always put on itself. It has claimed a continuous and enduring life of its own which enfolds all its members and distinguishes it from every other organization and from the totality of the worldly life outside of it. It is hard to deny this. Not only the Church as a whole, but distinctive groups and organizations within the Church, such as the Friends or the Jesuit Order, have maintained their own character and principles tenaciously against all influences. This is the noblest view that we can take of the Church, that the spirit of her Lord has always been an informing principle of life within her, and that, though faltering, sinning, and defiled, she has kept her own collective personality intact. Paul's discussion of the Church as the body of Christ (1 Cor. xii) is the first and classical discussion in Christian thought of the nature and functioning of a composite spiritual organism.

The Church is not the only organism of that kind, though pre-eminent among them all. Others are less permanent, less distinctive, less attractive, and less self-assertive, but the spiritual self-consciousness of the Church is built up on the social self-consciousness which it shares with other social organisms.

Josiah Royce, one of the ablest philosophical thinkers our nation has produced, has given us, in his " Problem of Christianity," his mature reflections on the subject of the Christian religion. The book is a great fragment, poorly balanced, confined in the main to a modern discussion of three great Pauline conceptions, sin, atonement, and the Church. The discussion of the Church is the ablest part of it; I shall return to that later. Following the lead of Wundt's Völkerpsychologie, Professor Royce was deeply impressed with the reality of super-personal forces in human life. He regards the comprehension of that fact as one of the most important advances in knowledge yet made.

"There are in the human world two profoundly different grades, or levels, of mental beings,— namely, the beings that we usually call human individuals, and the beings that we call communities.— Any highly organized community is as truly a human being as you and I are individually human. Only a community is not what we usually call an individual human being because it has no one separate and internally well-knit physical organism of its own; and because its mind, if you attribute to it any one mind, is therefore not manifested through the expressive movements of such a single separate human organism. Yet there are reasons for attributing to a community a mind of its own.— The communities are vastly more complex, and, in many ways, are also immeasurably more potent and enduring than are the individuals. Their mental life possesses, as Wundt has pointed out, a psychology of its own, which can be systematically studied. Their mental existence is no mere creation of abstract thinking or of metaphor; and is no more a topic for mystical insight, or for phantastic speculation, than is the mental existence of an individual man." [1]

This conception is of great importance for the doctrine of sin. I have spoken in the last chapter about the authority of the group over the individual within it, and its power to impose its own moral standard on its members, by virtue of which it educates them upward, if its standard is high, and debases them, if it is low. We need only mention some of the groups in our own national social life to realize how they vary in moral quality and how potent they are by virtue of their collective life: high school fraternities; any college community; a trade union; the I. W. W.; the Socialist party; Tammany Hall; any military organization; an officers' corps; the police force; the inside group of a local political party; the Free Masons; the Grange; the legal profession; a conspiracy like the Black Hand.

These super-personal forces count in the moral world not only through their authority over their members, but

[1] " Problem of Christianity," I, p. 164-167.

through their influence in the general social life. They front the world outside of them. Their real object usually lies outside. The assimilative power they exert over their members is only their form of discipline by which they bring their collective body into smooth and efficient working order. They are the most powerful ethical forces in our communities.

Evil collective forces have usually fallen from a better estate. Organizations are rarely formed for avowedly evil ends. They drift into evil under sinister leadership, or under the pressure of need or temptation. For instance, a small corrupt group in a city council, in order to secure control, tempts the weak, conciliates and serves good men, and turns the council itself into a force of evil in the city; an inside ring in the police force grafts on the vice trade, and draws a part of the force into protecting crime and brow-beating decent citizens; a trade union fights for the right to organize a shop, but resorts to violence and terrorizing; a trust, desiring to steady prices and to get away from antiquated competition, undersells the independents and evades or purchases legislation. This tendency to deterioration shows the soundness of the social instincts, but also the ease with which they go astray, and the need of righteous social institutions to prevent temptation.

In the previous chapter it was pointed out that the love of gain is one of the most unlimited desires and the most inviting outlet for sinful selfishness. The power of combination lends itself to extortion. Predatory profit or graft, when once its sources are opened up and developed, constitutes an almost overwhelming tempta-

tion to combinations of men. Its pursuit gives them
cohesion and unity of mind, capacity to resist common
dangers, and an outfit of moral and political principles
which will justify their anti-social activities. The aggressive and defensive doings of such combinations are
written all over history. History should be re-written
to explain the nature of human parasitism. It would
be a revelation. The Roman publicani, who collected
the taxes from conquered provinces on a contract basis;
the upper class in all slave-holding communities; the
landlord class in all ages and countries, such as East
Prussia, Ireland, Italy, and Russia; the great trading
companies in the early history of commerce; — these are
instances of social groups consolidated by extortionate
gain. Such groups necessarily resist efforts to gain
political liberty or social justice, for liberty and justice
do away with unearned incomes. Their malign influence on the development of humanity has been beyond
telling.

The higher the institution, the worse it is when it
goes wrong. The most disastrous backsliding in history
was the deterioration of the Church. Long before the
Reformation the condition of the Church had become
the most serious social question of the age. It weighed
on all good men. The Church, which was founded on
democracy and brotherhood, had, in its higher levels,
become an organization controlled by the upper classes
for parasitic ends, a religious duplicate of the coercive
State, and a chief check on the advance of democracy
and brotherhood. Its duty was to bring love, unity and
freedom to mankind; instead it created division, fo-

mented hatred, and stifled intellectual and social liberty. It is proof of the high valuation men put on the Church that its corruption seems to have weighed more heavily on the conscience of Christendom than the corresponding corruption of the State. At least the religious Revolution antedated the political Revolution by several centuries. To-day the Church is practically free from graft and exploitation; its sins are mainly sins of omission; yet the contrast between the idea of the Church and its reality, between the force for good which it might exert and the force which it does exert in public life, produces profounder feelings than the shortcomings of the State.

While these pages are being written, our nation is arming itself to invade another continent for the purpose of overthrowing the German government, on the ground that the existence of autocratic governments is a menace to the peace of the world and the freedom of its peoples. This momentous declaration of President Wilson recognizes the fact that the Governments of Great States too may be super-personal powers of sin; that they may in reality be only groups of men using their fellow-men as pawns and tools; that such governments have in the past waged war for dynastic and class interests without consulting the people; and that in their diplomacy they have cunningly contrived plans of deception and aggression, working them out through generations behind the guarded confidences of a narrow and privileged class.[1]

[1] These ideas and phrases are drawn from the President's Address to Congress on April 2nd, 1917.

There is no doubt that these charges justly characterize the German government. There is no doubt that
they characterize all governments of past history with
few exceptions, and that even the democratic governments of to-day are not able to show clean hands on
these points. The governments even of free States like
the Dutch Republic, the city republics of Italy, and the
British Empire have been based on a relatively narrow
group who determined the real policies and decisions of
the nation. How often have we been told that in our
own country we have one government on paper and
another in fact? Genuine political democracy will evidence its existence by the social, economic, and educational condition of the people. Generally speaking, city
slums, a spiritless and drunken peasantry, and a large
emigration are corollaries of class government. If the
people were free, they would stop exploitation. If they
can not stop exploitation, the parasitic interests are presumably in control of legislation, the courts, and the
powers of coercion. Parasitic government is sin on a
high scale. If this war leads to the downfall or regeneration of all governments which support the exploitation of the masses by powerful groups, it will be worth
its cost.

The social gospel realizes the importance and power
of the super-personal forces in the community. It has
succeeded in awakening the social conscience of the nation to the danger of allowing such forces to become
parasitic and oppressive. A realization of the spiritual
power and value of these composite personalities must
get into theology, otherwise theology will not deal ade-

quately with the problem of sin and of redemption, and will be unrelated to some of the most important work of salvation which the coming generations will have to do.

CHAPTER IX

THE KINGDOM OF EVIL

THIS chapter will be the last step in our discussion of the doctrine of sin. We have sought to show that in the following points a modification or expansion is needed in order to give the social gospel an intellectual basis and a full medium of expression in theology.

1. Theological teaching on the first origin of sin ought not to obscure the active sources of sin in later generations and in present-day life, by which sin is quickened and increased. An approximation to the reticence of Jesus and the prophets about the fall of man, and to their strong emphasis on the realistic facts of contemporary sin, would increase the practical efficiency of theology.

2. Since an active sense of failure and sin is produced by contrast with the corresponding ideal of righteousness, theology, by obscuring and forgetting the Kingdom of God has kept the Christian world out of a full realization of the social sins which frustrate the Kingdom. The social gospel needs above all a restoration of religious faith in the Reign of God in order to create an adequate sense of guilt for public sins, and it must look to theology to furnish the doctrinal basis of it.

3. The doctrine of original sin has directed attention to the biological channels for the transmission of general sinfulness from generation to generation, but has neg-

lected and diverted attention from the transmission and perpetuation of specific evils through the channels of social tradition.

4. Theology has not given adequate attention to the social idealizations of evil, which falsify the ethical standards for the individual by the authority of his group or community, deaden the voice of the Holy Spirit to the conscience of individuals and communities, and perpetuate antiquated wrongs in society. These social idealizations are the real heretical doctrines from the point of view of the Kingdom of God.

5. New spiritual factors of the highest significance are disclosed by the realization of the super-personal forces, or composite personalities, in society. When these backslide and become combinations for evil, they add enormously to the power of sin. Theology has utilized the terminology and results of psychology to interpret the sin and regeneration of individuals. Would it stray from its field if it utilized sociological terms and results in order to interpret the sin and redemption of these super-personal entities in human life?

The solidaristic spiritual conceptions which have been discussed must all be kept in mind and seen together, in order to realize the power and scope of the doctrine to which they converge: the Kingdom of Evil.

In some of our swampy forests the growth of ages has produced impenetrable thickets of trees and undergrowth, woven together by creepers, and inhabited by things that creep or fly. Every season sends forth new growth under the urge of life, but always developing from the old growth and its seeds, and still perpetuating the same rank mass of life. The life of humanity is infinitely interwoven, always renewing itself, yet always perpetuating what has been. The evils of one generation are caused by the wrongs of the generations that preceded, and will in turn condition the sufferings and temptations of those who come after. Our Italian immigrants are what they are because the Church and the land system of Italy have made them so. The Mexican peon is ridden by the Spanish past. Capitalistic Europe has fastened its yoke on the neck of Africa. When negroes are hunted from a Northern city like beasts, or when a Southern city degrades the whole nation by turning the savage inhumanity of a mob into a public festivity, we are continuing to sin because our fathers created the conditions of sin by the African slave trade and by the unearned wealth they gathered from slave labour for generations.

Stupid dynasties go on reigning by right of the long time they have reigned. The laws of the ancient Roman despotism were foisted by ambitious lawyers on mediaeval communities, to which they were in no wise fitted, and once more strangled liberty, and dragged free farmers into serfdom. When once the common land of a nation, and its mines and waters, have become the private property of a privileged band, nothing short of a social earthquake can pry them from their right of collecting private taxes. Superstitions which originated in the third century are still faithfully cultivated by great churches, compressing the minds of the young with fear and cherished by the old as their most precious

faith.   Ideas struck out by a wrestling mind in the heat
of an argument are erected by later times into proof-
texts more decisive than masses of living facts.   One
nation arms because it fears another; the other arms
more because this armament alarms it; each subsidizes
a third and a fourth to aid it.   Two fight; all fight;
none knows how to stop; a planet is stained red in a
solidarity of hate and horror.

The entomologist Fabre investigated the army caterpillar, which marches in dense thousands, apparently
under some leadership which all obey.   But Fabre found
there is no leadership.   Each simply keeps in touch with
the caterpillar just ahead of it and follows, follows on.
The one article of faith is to follow the leaders, though
none of the leaders knows whither they are going.   The
experimenter led the column to march in a circle by getting the front rank in touch with the rear, and now they
milled around helplessly like lost souls in Dante's hell.

If this were the condition of humanity, we should
be in a state of relative innocency and bliss.   The front-
rank caterpillars are at least not trying to make something out of the rest, and are not leading them to their
destruction by assuring them that they are doing it for
their good and for the highest spiritual possessions of
the caterpillar race.   Human society has leaders who
know what they want, but many of them have manipu-
lated the fate of thousands for their selfish ends.   The
sheep-tick hides in the wool of the sheep and taps the
blood where it flows warm and rich.   But the tick has
no power to alter the arterial system of the sheep and to
bring the aorta close to the skin where it can get at it.

Human ticks have been able to do this. They have gained control of legislation, courts, police, military, royalty, church, property, religion, and have altered the constitution of nations in order to make things easy for the tick class. The laws, institutions, doctrines, literature, art, and manners which these ruling classes have secreted have been social means of infection which have bred new evils for generations.

Any reader who doubts these sad statements can find the facts in the books, though mostly in foot-notes in fine print. It is also going on in real life. We can watch it if we look at any nation except our own.

This is what the modern social gospel would call the Kingdom of Evil. Our theological conception of sin is but fragmentary unless we see all men in their natural groups bound together in a solidarity of all times and all places, bearing the yoke of evil and suffering. This is the explanation of the amazing regularity of social statistics. A nation registers so and so many suicides, criminal assaults, bankruptcies, and divorces per 100,000 of the population. If the proportion changes seriously, we search for the disturbing social causes, just as we search for the physical causes if the rhythm of our pulse-beat runs away from the normal. The statistics of social morality are the pulse-beat of the social organism. The apparently free and unrelated acts of individuals are also the acts of the social group. When the social group is evil, evil is over all.

The conception of a Kingdom of Evil is not a new idea. It is as old as the Christian Church and older.

But while our modern conception is naturally historical and social, the ancient and mediaeval Church believed in a Kingdom of evil spirits, with Satan at their head, which is the governing power in the present world and the source of all temptation.

The belief in evil spirits is so common in ethnic religions that the relative absence of that belief in the Old Testament is proper cause for wonder. There are only a few passages referring to evil spirits, and a few referring to a spiritual being called Satan. It is altogether likely that the belief in dangerous and malicious spirits held a much larger place in the popular religious life of the Jewish people than we would gather from their literature. If the higher religious minds, who wrote the biblical books, purposely kept the popular beliefs down and out of sight, that gives remarkable support to those who regard the belief in personal evil spirits as a seamy and dangerous element of religion.

After the Exile the religion of the Jews was filled with angels and devils, each side built up in a great hierarchy, rank above rank. Evidently this systematized and theological belief in a satanic kingdom was absorbed from the Eastern religions with which the Jews came into close contact during the Exile. The monotheism of the Hebrew faith held its own against the dualism of the East, but the belief in Satan is a modified dualism compatible with the reign of Jehovah. The apocalyptic system is a theology built up on this semi-dualistic conception, describing the conflict of the Kingdom of Satan against God and his angels and his holy nation, and the final triumph of God.

The belief in the Satanic Kingdom and the apocalyptic theology were transferred from Judaism to Christianity as part of the initial inheritance of the new religion from the old, and any one familiar with patristic literature and with popular mediaeval religion needs no reminder that this was one of the most active and effective parts of the religious consciousness. The original belief was reinforced by the fact that all the gods and the daimonia of the Græco-Roman world were dyed black and classified as devils and evil spirits by the aggressive hostility of the Church. This process was repeated when the mediaeval Church was exorcising the pagan gods from the minds and customs of the Teutonic nations. All these gods remained realities, but black realities.

Popular superstition, systematized and reinforced by theology, and inculcated by all the teaching authority of the mediaeval Church, built up an overwhelming impression of the power of evil. The Christian spirit was thrown into an attitude of defence only. The best that could be done was to hold the powers of darkness at bay by the sign of the cross, by holy water, by sacred amulets, by prayer, by naming holy names. The church buildings and church yards were places of refuge from which the evil spirits were banned. The gargoyles of Gothic architecture are the evil spirits escaping from the church buildings because the spiritual power within is unbearable to them. I recently witnessed a corner-stone laying at a new Catholic church. The bishop and the clergy thrice moved in procession around the foundation walls, chanting; an acolyte carried a pailful of holy

water, and the bishop liberally applied it to the walls.
So the rectangle of masonry became an exempt and dis-
infected area of safety. Under the sunshine of an
American afternoon, and with a crowd of modern folks
around, it was an interesting survival.

The belief in a demonic Kingdom was in no wise attacked in the Reformation. Luther's sturdy belief in
devils is well known. Indeed, the belief which had
been built up for centuries by the Church, came to its
terrible climax during the age of the Reformation in the
witch trials. From A. D. 1400 to 1700, hundreds of
thousands of women and girls were imprisoned, tortured, and burned. These witch trials were grounded
on the belief in the satanic kingdom. Thomas Aquinas
furnished the theological basis; the Inquisition reduced
it to practice; Innocent VIII in 1484 in the bull *Sum-
mis desiderantes* lent it the highest authority of the
Church; the *Malleus Maleficarum* (1487 or 1488) codi-
fied it; lawyers, judges, informers, and executioners exploited it for gain; information given by malice, fear,
or the shrieks of the tortured made the contagion self-
perpetuating and ever spreading. It prevailed in
Protestant countries equally with Catholic. To believe
in the machinations of evil spirits and their compact
with witches was part of orthodoxy, part of profounder
piety. If the devil and his spirits are not real but a
figment of social imagination, yet at that time the devil
was real, just as real as any flesh and blood being and
far more efficient. Theology had made him real. The
Reformation theology did not end this craze of horror.
Aside from the humane religious spirit of a few who

wrote against it, it was the blessed scepticism of the
age of Enlightenment and the dawn of modern science
which saved humanity from the furies of a theology
which had gone wrong.

The passive and defensive attitude toward the satanic
Kingdom of Evil still continues wherever the belief in
evil spirits and in the apocalyptic theology is active.
Bunyan's " Pilgrim's Progress " presents a dramatic rec-
ord of the Calvinistic religious consciousness in its prime.
In all the wonderful adventures and redoubtable combats
of Christian and his companions and heavenly aids, they
are on the defensive. The only exception that I can remember occurs in the second part, when Christian's
wife and children, personally conducted by Great-Heart,
pass by Doubting Castle where Christian and Hopeful
were imprisoned by Giant Despair.

" So they sat down and consulted what was best to be done:
to wit, now they were so strong, and had got such a man as
Mr. Great-Heart for their conductor, whether they had not best
to make an attempt upon the giant, demolish his castle, and
if there were any pilgrims in it, to set them at liberty, before
they went any further. So one said one thing, and another
said the contrary. One questioned if it was lawful to go upon
unconsecrated ground; another said they might, provided their
end was good; but Mr. Great-Heart said, " Though that assertion offered last cannot be universally true, yet I have a commandment to resist sin, to overcome evil, to fight the good fight
of faith; and pray, with whom should I fight this good fight, if
not with Giant Despair? I will therefore attempt the taking
away of his life and the demolishing of Doubting Castle."

So they passed from the defensive to the offensive attitude and demolished the castle. The serious delibera-
tions of the party show that Bunyan realized that this

was a new departure. He was, in fact at that moment
parting company with the traditional attitude of theology and religion, and putting one foot hesitatingly
into the social gospel and the preventive methods of
modern science. Note that it was Mr. Great-Heart who
made the move.

To-day the belief in a satanic kingdom exists only
where religious and theological tradition keeps it alive.
It is not spontaneous, and it would not originate anew.
Its lack of vitality is proved by the fact that even those
who accept the existence of a personal Satan without
question, are not influenced in their daily life by the
practical belief in evil spirits. The demons have faded
away into poetical unreality. Satan alone remains, but
he has become a literary and theological devil, and most
often a figure of speech. He is a theological necessity
rather than a religious reality. He is needed to explain
the fall and the temptation, and he re-appears in eschatology. But our most orthodox theology on this point
would have seemed cold and sceptical to any of the
great theologians of the past.

No positive proof can be furnished that our universe
contains no such spiritual beings as Satan and his angels.
Impressive arguments have been made for their existence. The problem of evil is simplified if all is reduced to this source. But the fact confronts us,— and
I think it can not be denied,— that Satan and his angels
are a fading religious entity, and that a vital belief in
demon powers is not forthcoming in modern life.

In that case we can no longer realize the Kingdom of
Evil as a demonic kingdom. The live realization of this

belief will be confined to narrow circles, mostly of pre-millennialists; the Church would have to use up its precious moral authority in persuading its members to hold fast a belief which all modern life bids them drop. Yet we ought to get a solidaristic and organic conception of the power and reality of evil in the world. If we miss that, we shall see only disjointed facts. The social gospel is the only influence which can renew the idea of the Kingdom of Evil in modern minds, because it alone has an adequate sense of solidarity and a sufficient grasp of the historical and social realities of sin. In this modern form the conception would offer religious values similar to those of the old idea, but would not make such drafts on our credulity, and would not invite such unchristian superstitions and phantasms of fear.

The ancient demonic conception and the modern social conviction may seem at first sight to be quite alien to each other. In fact, however, they are blood-kin.

The belief in a Satanic kingdom, in so far as it was not merely theology but vital religious faith, has always drawn its vitality from political and social realities. The conception of an empire of evil fastened on Jewish thought after the Jews had an opportunity during the Exile to observe imperialism at close range and to be helpless under its power. The splendor of an Oriental court and its court language deeply influenced the Jewish conception of God. He was surrounded with a heavenly retinue, and despotic ideas and phraseology were applied. The same social experiences also enlarged the

conception of the reign of evil. The little evil spirits
had been enough to explain the evil of local Jewish
communities. But a great malign power was needed as
the religious backing of the oppressive international
forces in whose talons the Jewish race was writhing.
Satan first got his vitality as an international political
concept.

The political significance of the belief in the Satanic
kingdom becomes quite clear in the relation of the early
Church to the Roman Empire. The Apocalypse of
John is most enlightening on this fact. The Empire is
plainly described as the creature and agent of the Satanic
powers. The Beast with the seven heads had received
its dominion from the great Dragon. The great city,
which is described as the commercial and financial
centre of the world, falls with a crash when Satan and
his host are overthrown by the Messiah. Evidently the
political system of Rome and the demonic powers are
seen as the physical and spiritual side of the same evil
power.

Early Christianity is usually described as opposed to
paganism, and we think of the pagan religion as a rival
religious system. But it was also a great social force
penetrating all community life, the symbol of social coherence and loyalty. Its social usages let no one alone.
It became coercive and threatening where religious actions had political significance, especially in the worship
of the emperor. Christians believed the pagan gods to be
in reality demon powers, who had blinded and enticed
men to worship them. Whoever did worship them came
under their defiling power. Idolatry was an unforgiv-

able sin. All the life of the Church aimed to nerve
Christians to suffer anything rather than come under
the control of the dark powers again from which baptism had saved them. When the choice confronted them
and they were pinned to the wall, the hand that gripped
them was the hand of the Roman Empire, but the face
that leered at them was the face of the adversary of
God. So the belief in a Satanic kingdom of evil drew
its concrete meaning and vitality from social and political realities. It was their religious interpretation.

In the Middle Ages, when the Roman Empire had
become a great memory, the Papacy was the great international power, rich, haughty, luxurious, domineer-
ing, commanding the police powers of States for its
coercive purposes, and claiming the heritage of the em-
perors. The democratic movements which sprang up
during the eleventh and twelfth centuries and headed
toward a freer religion and a more fraternal social life,
found the papacy against them. Then the Apocalypse
took on new life. The city on the seven hills, drunk
with the blood of the saints, and clad in scarlet, was
still there. The followers of Jesus who suffered in the
grip of the international hierarchy did not see this
power as a Christian Church using oppressive measures,
but as an anti-christian power, the tool of Satan and
the adversary of God. This belief was inherited by
Protestantism and was one of its fighting weapons.
Once more it was a political and social reality which
put heat and vitality into the belief in the reign of Satan.

To-day there is no such world-wide power of oppression as the Roman Empire or the mediaeval papacy.

The popular superstitious beliefs in demonic agencies have largely been drained off by education. The conception of Satan has paled. He has become a theological devil, and that is an attenuated and precarious mode of existence. At the same time belief in original sin is also waning. These two doctrines combined,— the hereditary racial unity of sin, and the supernatural power of evil behind all sinful human action,— created a solidaristic consciousness of sin and evil, which I think is necessary for the religious mind. Take away these two doctrines, and both our sense of sin and our sense of the need of redemption will become much more superficial and will be mainly concerned with the transient acts and vices of individuals.

A social conception of the Kingdom of Evil, such as I have tried to sketch, makes a powerful appeal to our growing sense of racial unity. It is modern and grows spontaneously out of our livest interests and ideas. Instead of appealing to conservatives, who are fond of sitting on antique furniture, it would appeal to the radicals. It would contain the political and social protest against oppression and illusion for which the belief in a Satanic kingdom stood in the times of its greatest vitality. The practical insight into the solidarity of all nations in their sin would emphasize the obligation to share with them all every element of salvation we possess, and thus strengthen the appeal for missionary and educational efforts.

The doctrine of original sin was meant to bring us all under the sense of guilt. Theology in the past has labored to show that we are in some sense partakers of Adam's guilt. But the conscience of mankind has never been convinced. Partakers in his wretchedness we might well be by our family coherence, but guilt belongs only to personality, and requires will and freedom. On the other hand an enlightened conscience can not help feeling a growing sense of responsibility and guilt for the common sins under which humanity is bound and to which we all contribute. Who of us can say that he has never by word or look contributed to the atmospheric pressure of lubricious sex stimulation which bears down on young and old, and the effect of which after the war no man can predict without sickening? Whose hand has never been stained with income for which no equivalent had been given in service? How many business men have promoted the advance of democracy in their own industrial kingdom when autocracy seemed safer and more efficient? What nation has never been drunk with a sense of its glory and importance, and which has never seized colonial possessions or developed its little imperialism when the temptation came its way? The sin of all is in each of us, and every one of us has scattered seeds of evil, the final multiplied harvest of which no man knows.

At the close of his great invective against the religious leaders of his nation (Matth. xxiii), Jesus has a solidaristic vision of the spiritual unity of the generations. He warns his contemporaries that by doing over again the acts of their forefathers, they will bring upon them not only the blood they shed themselves, but the righteous blood shed long before. By solidarity of action and spirit we enter into solidarity of guilt. This applies to our spiritual unity with our contemporaries. If in the most restricted sphere of life we act on the same sinful principles of greed and tyranny on which the great exploiters and despots act, we share their guilt. If we consent to the working principles of the Kingdom of Evil, and do not counteract it with all our strength, but perhaps even fail to see its ruinous evil, then we are part of it and the salvation of Christ has not yet set us free.

I should like to quote, in closing this discussion, a remarkable passage from Schleiermacher's systematic theology, which describes the Kingdom of Evil without calling it by that name. I need not say that Schleiermacher was one of the really creative minds in the history of Protestant theology, a man who set new problems and made old problems profounder, thus fertilizing the thoughts even of those who know nothing of him. Speaking of the universal racial sin of humanity he said:

"If, now, this sinfulness which precedes all acts of sin, is produced in every individual through the sinful acts and condition of others; and if on the other hand every man by his own free actions propagates and strengthens it in others; then it is something wholly common to us (gemeinschaftlich). Whether we view this sinfulness as guilt and as conscious action, or as a principle and condition of life, in either aspect it is something wholly common, not pertaining to every individual separately or referring to him alone, but *in each the work of all, and in all the work of each.* In fact we can understand it justly and completely only in this solidarity. For that reason the doctrines dealing with it are never to be taken as expressions of individual self-consciousness, but they are expressions of the common consciousness. This solidarity is a unity of all places and all times. The peculiar form which this racial sinfulness takes in any individual, is simply an integral part of the form it takes in the social group to which he belongs, so that his sin is incomprehensible if taken alone and must always be taken in connection with the rest. This principle runs through all the concentric circles of solidaristic consciousness, through families, clans, tribes, nations, and races; the form which sinfulness takes in any of these can be understood only in connection with the rest. Therefore the total force exerted by the flesh against the spirit in all human actions incompatible with the consciousness of God, can be truly realized only when we see the totality of all contemporary life, never in any part alone. The same holds true of the succession of generations. The congenital sinfulness of one generation is conditioned by the sinfulness of those who preceded, and in turn conditions the sin of those who follow." [1]

Ritschl, another incisive and original theological thinker, adopted this solidaristic conception of sin, and its correlated ideas in the doctrine of salvation, as the basis of his theological system. He thinks that this,

[1] Schleiermacher, "Der Christliche Glaube," § 71, 2. 3d edition. The translation and italics are mine. A few unessential phrases are omitted to shorten the quotation.

and not the theory of subjective religion which is commonly quoted in connection with his name, is Schleiermacher's epoch-making contribution to theology.[1] Certainly the passage I have quoted shows what a capacity of religious vision is evoked by a religious comprehension of the solidarity of human life. " The consciousness of solidarity is one of the fundamental conditions of religion, without which it can neither be rightly understood nor rightly lived." [2]

[1] Ritschl, " Rechtfertigung und Versöhnung," I, p. 555.
[2] Ritschl, I, p. 496.

CHAPTER X

WE take up now the doctrine of salvation. All that has been said about sin will have to be kept in mind in discussing salvation, for the conceptions of sin and salvation are always closely correlated in every theological or religious system.

The new thing in the social gospel is the clearness and insistence with which it sets forth the necessity and the possibility of redeeming the historical life of humanity from the social wrongs which now pervade it and which act as temptations and incitements to evil and as forces of resistance to the powers of redemption. Its chief interest is concentrated on those manifestations of sin and redemption which lie beyond the individual soul. If our exposition of the superpersonal agents of sin and of the Kingdom of Evil is true, then evidently a salvation confined to the soul and its personal interests is an imperfect and only partly effective salvation.

Yet the salvation of the individual is, of course, an essential part of salvation. Every new being is a new problem of salvation. It is always a great and wonderful thing when a young spirit enters into voluntary obedience to God and feels the higher freedom with which Christ makes us free. It is one of the miracles of life. The burden of the individual is as heavy now as ever.

95

The consciousness of wrong-doing, of imperfection, of a wasted life lies on many and they need forgiveness and strength for a new beginning. Modern pessimism drains the finer minds of their confidence in the world and the value of life itself. At present we gasp for air in a crushing and monstrous world. Any return of faith is an experience of salvation.

Therefore our discussion can not pass personal salvation by. We might possibly begin where the old gospel leaves off, and ask our readers to take all the familiar experiences and truths of personal evangelism and religious nurture for granted in what follows. But our understanding of personal salvation itself is deeply affected by the new solidaristic comprehension furnished by the social gospel.

The social gospel furnishes new tests for religious experience. We are not disposed to accept the converted souls whom the individualistic evangelism supplies, without looking them over. Some who have been saved and perhaps reconsecrated a number of times are worth no more to the Kingdom of God than they were before. Some become worse through their revival experiences, more self-righteous, more opinionated, more steeped in unrealities and stupid over against the most important things, more devoted to emotions and unresponsive to real duties. We have the highest authority for the fact that men may grow worse by getting religion. Jesus says the Pharisees compassed sea and land to make a proselyte, and after they had him, he was twofold more a child of hell than his converters. To one whose memories run back twenty or thirty years, to Moody's time, the methods now used by some evangelists seem calculated to produce skin-deep changes. Things have simmered down to signing a card, shaking hands, or being introduced to the evangelist. We used to pass through some deep-soil ploughing by comparison. It is time to overhaul our understanding of the kind of change we hope to produce by personal conversion and regeneration. The social gospel furnishes some tests and standards.

but any methods?

When we undertook to define the nature of sin, we accepted the old definition, that sin is selfishness and rebellion against God, but we insisted on putting humanity into the picture. The definition of sin as selfishness gets its reality and nipping force only when we see humanity as a great solidarity and God indwelling in it. In the same way the terms and definitions of salvation get more realistic significance and ethical reach when we see the internal crises of the individual in connection with the social forces that play upon him or go out from him. The form which the process of redemption takes in a given personality will be determined by the historical and social spiritual environment of the man. At any rate any religious experience in which our fellow-men have no part or thought, does not seem to be a distinctively Christian experience.

If sin is selfishness, salvation must be a change which turns a man from self to God and humanity. His sinfulness consisted in a selfish attitude, in which he was at the centre of the universe, and God and all his fellowmen were means to serve his pleasures, increase his wealth, and set off his egotisms. Complete salvation, therefore, would consist in an attitude of love in which he would freely co-ordinate his life with the life of his fellows in obedience to the loving impulses of the spirit of God, thus taking his part in a divine organism of mutual service. When a man is in a state of sin, he may be willing to harm the life and lower the self-respect of a woman for the sake of his desires; he may be willing to take some of the mental and spiritual values out of the life of a thousand families, and lower the human level of a whole mill-town in order to increase his own dividends or maintain his autocratic sense of power. If this man came under the influence of the mind of Christ, he would see men and women as children of God with divine worth and beauty, and this realization would cool his lust or covetousness. Living now in the consciousness of the pervading spiritual life of God, he would realize that all his gifts and resources are a loan of God for higher ends, and would do his work with greater simplicity of mind and brotherliness. Of course in actual life there is no case of complete Christian transformation. It takes an awakened and regenerated mind a long time to find itself intellectually and discover what life henceforth is to mean to him, and his capacity for putting into practice what he knows he wants to do, will be something like the capacity of an untrained hand to express artistic imaginations. But in some germinal and rudimentary form salvation must turn us from a life centred on ourselves toward a life going out toward God and men. God is the all-embracing source and exponent of the common life and good of mankind. When we submit to God, we submit to the supremacy of the common good. Salvation is the voluntary socializing of the soul.

Conversion has usually been conceived as a break with our own sinful past. But in many cases it is also a break with the sinful past of a social group. Suppose a boy has been joining in cruel or lustful actions because his gang regards such things as fine and manly. If later he breaks with such actions, he will not only have to wrestle with his own habits, but with the social attractiveness and influence of his little humanity. If a working man becomes an abstainer, he will find out that intolerance is not confined to the good. In primitive Christianity baptism stood for a conscious break with pagan society. This gave it a powerful spiritual reaction. Conversion is most valuable if it throws a revealing light not only across our own past, but across the social life of which we are part, and makes our repentance a vicarious sorrow for all. The prophets felt so about the sins of their nation. Jesus felt so about Jerusalem, and Paul about unbelieving Israel.

We call our religious crisis " conversion " when we think of our own active break with old habits and associations and our turning to a new life. Paul introduced the forensic term "justification" into our religious vocabulary to express a changed legal status before God; his term " adoption " expresses the same change in terms derived from family life. We call the change "regeneration" when we think of it as an act of God within us, creating a new life.

only a holy real birth

The classical passage on regeneration (John iii) connects it with the Kingdom of God. Only an inward new birth will enable us to "see the Kingdom of God" and to "enter the Kingdom of God." The larger vision and the larger contact both require a new development of our spirit. In our unregenerate condition the consciousness of God is weak, occasional, and suppressed. The more Jesus Christ becomes dominant in us, the more does the light and life of God shine steadily in us, and create a religious personality which we did not have. Life is lived under a new synthesis.

It is strange and interesting that regeneration is thus connected with the Kingdom of God in John iii. The term has otherwise completely dropped out of the terminology of the fourth gospel. If we have here a verbatim memory of a saying of Jesus, the survival would indicate how closely the idea of personal regeneration was originally bound up with the Kingdom hope. When John the Baptist first called men to conversion and a change of mind, all his motives and appeals were taken from the outlook toward the Kingdom. Evidently the entire meaning of " conversion " and " regeneration " was subtly changed when the conception of the Kingdom disappeared from Christian thought. The change in ourselves was now no longer connected with a great divine change in humanity, for which we must prepare and get fit. If we are converted, what are we converted to? If we are regenerated, does the scope of so divine a transformation end in our " going to heaven "? The nexus between our religious experience and humanity seems gone when the Kingdom of God is not present in the idea of regeneration.

Through the experience and influence of Paul the word " faith " has gained a central place in the terminology of salvation. Its meaning fluctuates according to the dominant conception of religion. With Paul it was a comprehensive mystical symbol covering his whole inner experience of salvation and emancipation, which flooded his soul with joy and power. On the other hand wherever doctrine becomes rigid and is the pre-eminent thing in religion, " faith " means submission of the mind to the affirmations of dogma and theology, and, in particular, acceptance of the plan of salvation and trust in the vicarious atonement of Christ. Where the idea of the Church dominates religion, " faith " means mainly submission to the teaching and guidance of the Church. In popular religion it may shrivel up to something so small as putting a finger on a Scripture text and "claiming the promise."

In primitive Christianity the forward look of expectancy was characteristic of religion. The glory of the coming dawn was on the Eastern clouds. This influenced the conception of " faith." It was akin to hope, the forward gaze of the pioneers. The historical illustrations of faith in Hebrews xi show faith launching life toward the unseen future.

This is the aspect of faith which is emphasized by the social gospel. It is not so much the endorsement of ideas formulated in the past, as expectancy and confidence in the coming salvation of God. In this respect the forward look of primitive Christianity is resumed. Faith once more means prophetic vision. It is faith to assume that this is a good world and that life is worth living. It is faith to assert the feasibility of a fairly righteous and fraternal social order. In the midst of a despotic and predatory industrial life it is faith to stake our business future on the proposition that fairness, kindness, and fraternity will work. When war inflames a nation, it is faith to believe that a peaceable disposition is a workable international policy. Amidst the disunion of Christendom it is faith to look for unity and to express unity in action. It is faith to see God at work in the world and to claim a share in his job. Faith is an energetic act of the will, affirming our fellowship with God and man, declaring our solidarity with the Kingdom of God, and repudiating selfish isolation.

"Sanctification," according to almost any definition, is the continuation of that process of spiritual education and transformation, by which a human personality becomes a willing organ of the spirit of Christ. Those who believe in the social gospel can share in any methods for the cultivation of the spiritual life, if only they have an ethical outcome. The social gospel takes up the message of the Hebrew prophets, that ritual and emotional religion is harmful unless it results in righteousness. Sanctification is through increased fellowship with God and man. But fellowship is impossible without an exchange of service. Here we come back to our previous proposition that the Kingdom of God is the commonwealth of co-operative service and that the most common form of sinful selfishness is the effort to escape from labor. Sanctification, therefore, can not be attained in an unproductive life, unless it is unproductive through necessity. In the long run the only true way to gain moral insight, self-discipline, humility, love, and a consciousness of coherence and dependence, is to take our place among those who serve one another by useful labor. Parasitism blinds; work reveals.

honest work

The fact that the social gospel is a distinct type of religious experience is proved by comparing it with mysticism. In most other types of Christianity the mystic experience is rated as the highest form of sanctification. In Catholicism the monastic life is the way of perfection, and mystic rapture is the highest attainment and reward of monastic contemplation and service. In Protestantism, which has no monastic leisure for mystic exercises, mysticism is of a homelier type, but in almost every group of believers there are some individuals who profess to have attained a higher stage of sanctification through "a second blessing," "the higher life," "complete sanctification," "perfect love," Christian science, or Theosophy. The literature and organizations ministering to this mystical life, go on the assumption that it far transcends the ordinary way in spiritual blessings and sanctifying power.

mysticism

Mysticism is a steep short-cut to communion with God. There is no doubt that under favorable conditions it has produced beautiful results of unselfishness, humility, and undauntable courage. Its danger is that it isolates. In energetic mysticism the soul concentrates on God, shuts

out the world, and is conscious only of God and itself.
In its highest form, even the consciousness of self is
swallowed up in the all-filling possession of God. No
wonder it is absorbing and wonderful. But we have
to turn our back on the world to attain this experience,
and when we have attained it, it makes us indifferent to
the world. What does Time matter when we can live
in Eternity? What gift can this world offer us after
we have entered into the luminous presence of God?

The mystic way to holiness is not through humanity
but above it. We can not set aside the fundamental law
of God that way. He made us for one another, and our
highest perfection comes not by isolation but by love.
The way of holiness through human fellowship and service is slower and lowlier, but its results are more essentially Christian. Paul dealt with the mystic phenomena
of religion when he dealt with the charismata of primitive Christianity, especially with glossolalia (1 Cor.
xii–xiv). It is a striking fact that he ranks the spiritual gifts not according to their mystic rapture, but according to their rational control and their power of serving others. His great chapter on love dominates the
whole discussion and is offered as a counter-poise and
antidote to the dangers of mysticism.[1]

Mysticism is not the maturest form of sanctification.

[1] I have set this forth fully in my little book, "Dare We Be
Christians?" (Pilgrim Press, Boston.) In my "Prayers of the
Social Awakening" (Pilgrim Press), I have tried to connect the
social consciousness with the devotional life by prayers envision-
ing social groups and movements. Professor Herrmann's "The
Communion of the Christian with God" deals with the difference
of the mystic way and the way of service.

As Professor Royce well says: " It is the always young, it is the childlike, it is the essentially immature aspect of the deeper religious life. Its ardor, its pathos, its illusions, and its genuine illuminations have all the characters of youth about them, characters beautiful, but capricious." [1] There is even question whether mysticism proper, with rapture and absorption, is Christian in its antecedents, or Platonic.

I believe in prayer and meditation in the presence of God; in the conscious purging of the soul from fear, love of gain, and selfish ambition, through realizing God; in bringing the intellect into alignment with the mind of Christ; and in re-affirming the allegiance of the will to the Kingdom of God. When a man goes up against hard work, conflict, loneliness, and the cross, it is his right to lean back on the Eternal and to draw from the silent reservoirs. But what we get thus is for use. Personal sanctification must serve the Kingdom of God. Any mystic experience which makes our fellow-men less real and our daily labour less noble, is dangerous religion. A religious experience is not Christian unless it binds us closer to men and commits us more deeply to the Kingdom of God.

Thus the fundamental theological terms about the experiences of salvation get a new orientation, correction, and enrichment through the religious point of view contained in the social gospel. These changes would effect an approximation to the spirit and outlook of primitive Christianity, going back of Catholicism and Protestantism alike.

[1] Royce, " Problem of Christianity," I, p. 400.

The definitions we have attempted are not merely academic and hypothetical exercises. Religion is actually being experienced in such ways.

In the Bible we have several accounts of religious experiences which were fundamental in the life of its greatest characters. A few are told in their own striking phrases. Others are described by later writers, and in that case indicate what popular opinion expected such men to experience. Now, none of these experiences, so far as I see, are of that solitary type in which a soul struggles for its own salvation in order to escape the penalties of sin or to attain perfection and peace for itself. All were experienced with a conscious outlook toward humanity. When Moses saw the glory of God in the flaming bush and learned the ineffable name of the Eternal, it was not the salvation of Moses which was in question but the salvation of his people from the bondage of Egypt. When young Samuel first heard the call of the Voice in the darkness, it spoke to him of priestly extortion and the troubled future of his people. When Isaiah saw the glory of the Lord above the Cherubim, he realized by contrast that he was a man of unclean lips, but also that he dwelt among a people of unclean lips. His cleansing and the dedication which followed were his preparation for taking hold of the social situation of his nation. In Jeremiah we are supposed to have the attainment of the religion of the individual, but even his intimate experiences were all in full view of the fate of his nation. Paul's experience at Damascus was the culmination of his personal struggle and his emergence into spiritual freedom. But his crisis got its intensity from its social background. He was deciding, so far as he was concerned, between the old narrow nationalistic religion of conservative Judaism and a wider destiny for his people, between the validity of the Law and spiritual liberty, between the exclusive claims of Israel on the Messianic hope and a world-wide participation in the historical prerogatives of the first-born people. The issues for which his later life stood were condensed in the days at Damascus, as we can see from his own recital in Galatians i, and these religious issues were the fundamental social questions for his nation at that time.

We can not afford to rate this group of religious experiences at a low value. As with us all, the theology of the prophets was based on their personal experiences. Out of them grew their ethical monotheism and their God-consciousness. This was the highest element in the spiritual heritage of his people which came to Jesus. He re-interpreted and perfected it in his personality, and in that form it has remained the highest factor among the various historical strains combined in our religion.

These prophetic experiences were not superficial. There was soul-shaking emotion, a deep sense of sin, faith in God, longing for him, self-surrender, enduement with spiritual power. Yet they were not ascetic, not individualistic, not directed toward a future life. They were social, political, solidaristic.

The religious experiences evoked by the social gospel belong to the same type, though deeply modified, of course, by the profound differences between their age and ours. What the wars and oppressions of Israel and Judah meant to them, the wars and exploitations of mod-

ern civilization mean to us. In these things God speaks
to our souls. When we face these questions we meet
God. An increasing number of young men and women,
— and some of the best of them — are getting their call
to repentance, to a new way of life, and to the conquest
of self in this way, and a good many older men are su-
perimposing a new experience on that of their youth.

Other things being equal, a solidaristic religious experience is more distinctively Christian than an individualistic religious experience. To be afraid of hell or
purgatory and desirous of a life without pain or trouble
in heaven was not in itself Christian. It was self-inter-
est on a higher level. It is not strange that men were
wholly intent on saving themselves as long as such dangers as Dante describes were real to their minds. A man
might be pardoned for forgetting his entire social consciousness if he found himself dangling over a blazing
pit. But even in more spiritual forms of conversion,
as long as men are wholly intent on their own destiny,
they do not necessarily emerge from selfishness. It only
changes its form. A Christian regeneration must have
an outlook toward humanity and result in a higher social
consciousness.

The saint of the future will need not only a theocen-
tric mysticism which enables him to realize God, but an
anthropocentric mysticism which enables him to realize
his fellow-men in God. The more we approach pure
Christianity, the more will the Christian signify a man
who loves mankind with a religious passion and excludes
none. The feeling which Jesus had when he said, "I am

the hungry, the naked, the lonely," will be in the emotional consciousness of all holy men in the coming days. The sense of solidarity is one of the distinctive marks of the true followers of Jesus.

CHAPTER XI

IN discussing the doctrine of sin we faced the fact that redemption will have to deal not only with the weakness of flesh and blood, but with the strength of principalities and powers.[1] Beyond the feeble and short-lived individual towers the social group as a super-personal entity, dominating the individual, assimilating him to its moral standards, and enforcing them by the social sanctions of approval or disapproval.

When these super-personal forces are based on an evil principle, or directed toward an evil purpose, or corrupted by some controlling group interest which is hostile to the common good, they are sinners of sublimer mould, and they block the way of redemption. They are to us what demonic personalities were to earlier Christian minds. Men of religious vision have always seen social communities in that way. The prophets dealt with Israel and Judah, with Moab and Assyria, as with personalities having a continuous life and spirit and destiny. Jesus saw Jerusalem as a man might see a beloved woman who is driven by haughtiness and self-will into tragic ruin.

In our age these super-personal social forces present more difficult problems than ever before. The scope

[1] Chapter VIII.

and diversity of combination is becoming constantly greater. The strategy of the Kingdom of God is short-sighted indeed if it does not devote thought to their salvation and conversion.

The salvation of the composite personalities, like that of individuals, consists in coming under the law of Christ. A few illustrations will explain how this applies.

Two principles are contending with each other for future control in the field of industrial and commercial organization, the capitalistic and the co-operative. The effectiveness of the capitalistic method in the production of wealth is not questioned; modern civilization is evidence of it. But we are also familiar with capitalistic methods in the production of human wreckage. Its one-sided control of economic power tempts to exploitation and oppression; it directs the productive process of society primarily toward the creation of private profit rather than the service of human needs; it demands autocratic management and strengthens the autocratic principle in all social affairs; it has impressed a materialistic spirit on our whole civilization.

On the other hand organizations formed on the co-operative principle are not primarily for profit but for the satisfaction of human wants, and the aim is to distribute ownership, control, and economic benefits to a large number of co-operators.

The difference between a capitalistic organization and a co-operative comes out clearly in the distribution of voting power. Capitalistic joint stock companies work on the plan of " one share, one vote." Therewith power is located in money. One crafty person who has a hundred shares can outvote ninety-nine righteous men who have a share apiece, and a small minority can outvote all the rest if it holds a majority of stock. Money is stronger than life, character, and personality.

Co-operatives work on the plan of " one man, one vote." A man who holds one share has as much voting power as a man with ten shares; his personality counts. If a man wants to lead and direct, he can not do it by money power; he must do it by character, sobriety, and good judgment. The small stockholders are not passive; they take part; they must be persuaded and taught. The superior ability of the capable can not outvote the rest, but has to train them. Consequently the co-operatives develop men and educate a community in helpful loyalty and comradeship. This is the advent of true democracy in economic life. Of course the co-operative principle is not a sovereign specific; the practical success of a given association depends on good judgment and the loyalty of its constituents. But the co-operatives, managed by plain men, often with little experience, have not only held their own in Europe against the picked survivors of the capitalistic competitive battle, but have forged steadily ahead into enormous financial totals, have survived and increased even during the war, and by their helpful moral influence have gone a long way to restore a country like Ireland which had long been drained and ruined by capitalism.

Here, I think, we have the difference between saved and unsaved organizations. The one class is under the law of Christ, the other under the law of mammon. The

one is democratic and the other autocratic. Whenever
capitalism has invaded a new country or industry, there
has been a speeding up in labor and in the production of
wealth, but always with a trail of human misery, discon-
tent, bitterness, and demoralization. When co-operation has invaded a country there has been increased thrift,
education, and neighborly feeling, and there has been no
trail of concomitant evil and no cries of protest. The
men in capitalistic business may be the best of men, far
superior in ability to the average committee member of
a co-operative, but the latter type of organization is the
higher, and when co-operation has had as long a time
to try out its methods as capitalism, the latter will rank
with feudalism as an evil memory of mankind.

  Super-personal forces are saved when they come under
the law of Christ. A State which uses its terrible power
of coercion to smite and crush offenders as a protection
to the rest, is still under brutal law. A State which
deals with those who have erred in the way of teaching,
discipline, and restoration, has come under the law of
Christ and is to that extent a saved community. " By
their fruits ye shall know them." States are known by
their courts and prisons and contract labor systems, or
by their juvenile courts and parole systems. A change
in penology may be an evidence of salvation.

  A State which uses its superior power to overrun a
weaker neighbor by force, or to wrest a valuable right
of way from it by instigating a *coup d'état,* or uses in-
timidation to secure mining or railway concessions or to
force a loan at usurious rates on a half-civilized State, is
in mortal sin. A State which asks only for an open door

and keeps its own door open in return, and which speaks as courteously to a backward State as to one with a big fleet, is to that extent a Christian community.[1]

With composite personalities as with individuals " the love of money is the root of all evil." Communities and nations fall into wild fits of anger and cruelty; they are vain and contemptuous of others; they lie and love lies; they sin against their critical conscience; they fall in love with virile and magnetic men just as women do. These are the temptations and dangers which every democracy will meet and from which it will recover with loss and some shame. But, as has been said before, evils become bold and permanent when there is money in them. It was the need of protecting wealth against poverty which made the courts and the criminal law so cruel in the past. It was theological superstition which started the epidemic of witch trials in Europe, but it was the large fees that fell to the lawyers and informers which made that craze so enduring. Nearly all modern wars have had their origin in the covetousness of trade and finance.[2]

If unearned gain is the chief corrupter of professions, institutions, and combinations of men, these super-personal beings will be put on the road to salvation when their graft is in some way cut off and they are compelled to subsist on the reward of honest service.

The history of the Church furnishes a striking exam-

---

[1] This matter of saving the community life has been discussed more fully in my book, " Christianizing the Social Order," the Macmillan Company, 1912.

[2] See historical instances in F. C. Howe, " Why War? "

ple. For generations before the Reformation the condition of the Church and of the ministry was the sorest
social question of the time, weighing heavily on the
conscience of all good men. The ministrations of the
Church, the sacrament of the altar, the merit gained by
the sacrifice of the mass, the penitential system, the practice of indulgences, had been turned into means of great
income to the Church and those who were in control of
it. The rank and file of the priests and monks were from
the common people, and their incomes were poor. But
the higher positions of the Church and the wealthier monasteries were in possession of the upper classes, who
filled the lucrative places with their younger sons or un-
married daughters. Where rich sinecures existed and an
immense patronage was in the gift of the higher churchmen, the rake-off was naturally practised and perfected.
Everyone who had paid for getting his position, recouped
his investment. The highest institution of service had
become the most glaring example of graft. Since the
Church always resisted the interference of the laity,
and since the oligarchy which surrounded the papacy was
itself the chief beneficiary of the ecclesiastical graft, re-
form was successfully blocked out, or quickly lapsed when
it was attempted.

It was this profit system in the Church which produced
the religious unrest and finally the revolutionary upheaval
of the Reformation in some nations. Men were not dis-
satisfied with the doctrines of the Church. There were
surprisingly few theological heretics. Wycliffe and his
followers are the only ones that gained popular influence,
and his chief interest, too, was in the social utilization of

the wealth of the Church.   Men like Savonarola were not
doctrinal reformers, but were trying to cleanse the Church
of its graft and the resulting idleness and vice.   The ideal
of " the poverty of the Church," which was common to
men so unlike as Saint Bernard, Arnold of Brescia, Saint
Francis, and all the democratic sects, must be understood
over against the vested wealth, the graft, and the semi-
governmental power of the Church.   They wanted the
Church voluntarily to give up its wealth, and to put its
ministers on the basis of service and the daily bread.

The Church refused to take this heroic path of repentance of its own free will.   So it was compelled to
take it.   In all the countries which officially adopted the
Reformation, the possessions and vested incomes of the
Church were secularized.   The sinecures mostly disappeared.   The bishops lost their governmental functions.
Everywhere the reform movements converged on this
impoverishment of the Church with a kind of collective
instinct.   Luther's theses on indulgences got their popularity not by their new and daring theology, for they were
a hesitating and wavering statement of a groping mind,—
but by the fact that they touched one of the chief sources
of papal income.   Several of the great doctrines of the
Reformation got their vitality by their internal connection with the question of church property.

The process of reformation which stripped the Church
of its landed wealth and privileges was nothing beautiful.
It was high-class looting.   Only a small portion of the
wealth was used to endow education and charity.   Most
of it was seized by kings, princes, and nobles.   This gave
a new lease of life to autocracy, and in England set up

some of the splendid aristocratic families, who still consume what was once given to God. But this unholy procedure did cleanse the Church and its ministry of graft. When there were few large incomes, the rake-off perforce ceased. A body of ministers developed who were on the whole educated, clean, and willing to serve to the best of their understanding on a meagre salary. A great profession had been saved. Its salvation did not come from theology, as theology would have us believe. Where the Roman Catholic clergy is on the basis of hard work and plain income, it has shown similar improvement. The remedy which purified the ministry and the Church "so as by fire," was that "poverty of the Church" which the medieval reformers had demanded. The average minister will not be in doubt that he has married the Lady Poverty, and that this keeps him from wantonness.

The salvation of the super-personal beings is by coming under the law of Christ. The fundamental step of repentance and conversion for professions and organizations is to give up monopoly power and the incomes derived from legalized extortion, and to come under the law of service, content with a fair income for honest work. The corresponding step in the case of governments and political oligarchies, both in monarchies and in capitalistic semi-democracies, is to submit to real democracy. Therewith they step out of the Kingdom of Evil into the Kingdom of God.

CHAPTER XII

THE CHURCH AS THE SOCIAL FACTOR OF SALVATION

WHAT is the function of the Church in the process of salvation? What is it worth to a man to have the support and guidance of the Church in saving his soul?

If we listen to the Church's own estimate of itself it is worth as much as oxygen is to animal life. It is indispensable. "Outside of the Church there is no salvation." Very early in its history the Church began to take a deep interest in itself and to assert high things about itself. Every community is inclined to develop an expanded self-consciousness if the opportunity is at all favorable, and the Christian Church has certainly not let its opportunity go begging. Some historian has said, it is a wonder that the Church has not been made a person in the Godhead.

It is important to remember that when its high claims were first developed, they were really largely true. Christianity was in sharp opposition not only to the State but to the whole social life surrounding it. It created a Christian duplicate of the social order for its members, as far as it could. Christian influences were not yet diffused in society and literature. The Christian spirit and tradition could really be found nowhere except in the organized Christian groups. If the individual was to be impregnated with the saving power of Christianity, the Church had to do it. There was actually no salvation outside of the Church. But the statements in which men of the first generations expressed their genuine experience of what the Church meant to them, were turned into a theological formula and repeated in later times when the situation had changed, and when, for a time, the Church was not the supreme help but a great hindrance. The claims for the indispensability of the Church and its sacraments and officers became more specific as the hierarchic Church developed. First no man could be saved outside of the Church; next he could not be saved unless he was in right relation to his bishop; and finally he could not be saved unless he submitted to the Roman pontiff.

What are the functions of the Church in salvation, and how indispensable is it? And what has the social gospel to say to the theological valuation of the Church?

The Church is the social factor in salvation. It brings social forces to bear on evil. It offers Christ not only many human bodies and minds to serve as ministers of his salvation, but its own composite personality, with a collective memory stored with great hymns and Bible stories and deeds of heroism, with trained aesthetic and moral feelings, and with a collective will set on righteousness. A super-personal being organized around an evil principle and set on predatory aims is the most potent breeder of sin in individuals and in other communities. What, then, might a super-personal being do which would be organized around Jesus Christ as its impelling power, and would have for its sole or chief object to embody his spirit in its life and to carry him into human thought and the conduct of affairs?

If there had never been such an organization as the Christian Church, every great religious mind would dream of the possibility of creating something like it. He would imagine the happy life within it where men shared the impulses of love and the convictions about life which Jesus imparted to humanity. If he understood psychology and social science, he would see the possibilities of such a social group in arousing and guiding the unformed spiritual aspirations of the young and reinforcing wayward consciences by the approval or disapproval of the best persons, and its power of reaching by free loyalty springs of action and character lying too deep for civil law and even for education to stir. He might well imagine too how the presence of such a social group would quicken and balance the civil and political community.

How far the actualities of church life fall short of such an ideal forecast, most of us know but too well. But even so, the importance of the social factor in salvation is clear from whatever angle we look at it. What chance would a disembodied spirit of Christianity have, whispering occasionally at the key-hole of the human heart? Nothing lasts unless it is organized, and if it is organized of human life, we must put up with the qualities of human life in it.

Within the field it has chosen to cultivate, the local church under good leadership is really a power of salvation. During the formative years of our national growth the churches gathered up the available resources of education, history, philosophy, eloquence, art, and music, and established social centres controlled by the highest possessions known to people whose other resources were the family, money, gossip, the daily paper, and the inevitable vices. The great ideas of the spiritual life — God, the soul, duty, sin, holiness, eternity — would today be wholly absent in many minds, and in most others would be but flickering lights, if the local churches did not cherish and affirm them, and make them glorious and persuasive by the most effective combination of social influences ever accumulated by any organization during a history lasting for centuries and spread through many nations.

We are so accustomed to the churches that we hardly realize what a social force they exert over the minds they do influence. If we could observe a native Christian church in a pagan people, after the Christian organization is once in operation as a social organism, and is weaning families and village communities from pagan customs and assimilating them to the new ideas, we should realize better the power of conservation exerted in our own communities.[1] The new religion of Christian Science provides another chance for such a realization. It expounds a new religious book alongside of the Bible, and a new prophet alongside of Christ, and thus creates a novel religious consciousness among its own people. It has taken many nervous, unhappy, and burdened persons, and has given health to their bodies and calmness and

[1] "Social Christianity in the Orient," by Emma Rauschenbusch Clough, Ph.D. (Macmillan Company) is a striking narrative of the revolutionary effect of the introduction of Christianity in an Indian pariah tribe.

self-control to their minds by attacking and subduing
their souls with a dogmatic faith, till they learn to contradict the rheumatic facts of life and to ignore even
the presence of death by looking the other way.   If we
could see the old churches as clearly as we see this new
church, we should realize their power.

The men who stand for the social gospel have been
among the most active critics of the churches because
they have realized most clearly both the great needs of
our social life and the potential capacities of the Church
to meet them.   Their criticism has been a form of com-
pliment to the Church.   I think they may yet turn out to
be the apologists whom the Church most needs at present.
They are best fitted to see that while the Church influences society, society has always influenced the Church,
and that the Church, when it has dropped to the level of
its environment, has simply yielded to the law of social
gravitation.   This is true of the delinquencies of the
Church in past ages, which lie heavily on our minds when
we want to describe the Church as the great organism of
salvation.   Those whose expectations are created by the
claims of the Church about itself may well be profoundly
disappointed when they go through some of the bad
chapters of Church History.   If they have to judge it
by its own absolute religious criteria as the body of
Christ and the exponent of his spirit, the gap between
the ideal and the reality is painful.   The fact is that the
Church has watered its own stock and can not pay dividends on all the paper it has issued.   It has made claims
for itself to which no organization composed of humans
can live up.   If we see it simply as an attempt to give

social expression to the life derived from Christ, we shall not feel too deeply disappointed when we see it fail. True social insight knows that its sins were always the sins of the age. If the Church was autocratic and oppressive, so were all governments. There was graft in the Church, but the feudal aristocracy was founded on graft, and it never fought it as the Church fought simony.

A fresh understanding for the indispensableness of the Church is gaining ground today in Protestant theology in spite of the increased knowledge of the past and present failures of the Church. This is an attempt to overcome the exaggerated individualism into which Protestantism was thrust by the violent reactions of the Reformation. When men were in the throes of a revolution against a Church which claimed everything, they naturally denied every claim by which the enemy could brace its authority. They denied the authority of the tradition and decrees of the Church and made the Bible the sole source of truth. They denied the doctrine of the eucharist because the mass was the chief monopoly right from which the Church drew material income and spiritual reverence. They emphasized and elaborated the doctrine of election because it effectively eliminated the middle-man in salvation; for it put man into direct contact with the source of salvation, and made the decree of salvation wholly independent of any human act or church mediation. But the result of this great polemical reaction against the Church was a system of religious individualism in which the social forces of salvation were slighted, and God and the individual were almost the only realities in sight.

Of course in actual practice the Protestant churches exercised very stout control over their members. Calvin, in a celebrated passage of the Institutes comes close to a social appreciation of the functions of the Church:

"But, as it is now our purpose to discourse of the visible Church, let us learn, from her single title of Mother, how useful, nay, how necessary the knowledge of her is, since there is no other means of entering into life unless she conceive us in the womb and give us birth, unless she nourish us at her breasts, and, in short, keep us under her charge and government, until, divested of mortal flesh, we become like the angels.— Moreover, beyond the pale of the Church no forgiveness of sins, no salvation, can be hoped for, as Isaiah and Joel testify.— The paternal favour of God and the special evidence of spiritual life are confined to his peculiar people, and hence the abandonment of the Church is always fatal." [1]

But all of us who have had to acquire our social and historical comprehension laboriously will appreciate how little the old Protestant system stimulated and developed the understanding of the social factor in redemption.

The individualism of Reformation theology is being overcome by a new insistence on the importance of the Church. This trend of thought is not due, as in Anglican theology, to a renascence of Catholicism, but to a combination of purified Protestantism and modern social insight. I have been struck by the eminence of some of the prophets of this new solidaristic strain in theology.

Schleiermacher in his earlier "Reden über die Religion" still interpreted the religious sense of dependence as an individual experience. Maturer reflection showed him that all personal life is determined by the spirit of the community with which it is organically con-

[1] Calvin, "Institutes of the Christian Religion," Book IV, i, 4.

nected. This is true of the religious life too. Our sin is due to the feebleness with which we realize God. Jesus lived in complete and unbroken consciousness of God. Contact with him can so strengthen the God-consciousness in us that we are able to overcome the power of sin and rise to newness of life. But the memory of his life and the consciousness of salvation in him are transmitted to us only by the Church. We share his consciousness by sharing the common faith and experience of the Church. The new life of the individual is mediated by the social organism which is already in possession of that life.

"The Protestant theology of our age rests on the foundation laid by Schleiermacher; all theologians — some directly, some more indirectly — are seeking to establish the connections between the religious personality of the individual and the common consciousness of the Church." [1]

Ritschl, the most vigorous and influential theological intellect in Germany since Schleiermacher, is evidence of this. He abandoned the doctrine of original sin but substituted the solidaristic conception of the Kingdom of Evil. He held that salvation is embodied in a community which has experienced salvation; the faith of the individual is part of the faith of the Church. The Church and not the individual is the object of justification, the assurance of forgiveness for the individual is based on his union with the Church.

In American thought the most striking utterance on the indispensable importance of the Church in salvation

[1] Pfleiderer, Glaubens-und Sittenlehre. § 55.

has come from an eminent outsider, a philosopher and not a theologian, Professor Royce. He had worked out "the philosophy of loyalty" in other fields, and then applied it to religion in "the Problem of Christianity" (1913). This book is the mature product of his life, and its argument is evidently uplifted by the conviction that he had discovered some highly important facts.

Professor Royce, as has been said before, held that there are in the human world two profoundly different grades or levels of mental beings, namely individuals and communities, and he calls it the most significant of all moral and religious truths "that a community, when unified by an active, indwelling purpose, is an entity more concrete and less mysterious than any individual man, and can love and be loved as a husband and wife love." What is love between man and man, becomes loyalty when it goes out from a man to his community.

Professor Royce felt profoundly on the sin of the individual. "The individual human being is by nature subject to some overwhelming moral burden, from which, if unaided, he can not escape. Both because of what has been technically called original sin, and because of the sins that he himself has committed, the individual is doomed to a spiritual ruin from which only a divine intervention can save him." (Lecture III.) He "cannot unaided win the true goal of life. Help must come to him from some source above his own level."

The individual is saved, if at all, by membership in a community which has salvation. When a man becomes loyal to a community, he identifies himself with its life; he appropriates its past history and memories, its experi-

ences and hopes, and absorbs its spirit and faith. This
is the power which can lift him above his own level.

The Christian religion possesses such a community.
It first comes into full view in the Pauline epistles. How
it originated is a mystery like the origin of life, for loyalty is always evoked by the loyalty of those who already
have it. Paul did not create it; he only formulated its
ideas.

Professor Royce thinks the creation of the Church was
the most important event in the history of Christianity.
Not Christ but the Church is the central idea of Christianity. He rates Jesus largely as an indispensable basis
on which the Church could form and stand. He thinks
we know little about him, and that Jesus defined the
Christian ideas inadequately. But his name was the
great symbol of loyalty for the Church. The doctrines
about him were developed because they were necessary
for the consolidation of the Church.

This slighting of Jesus is one of the most unsatisfactory elements in Royce's thought. If the awakening of
loyalty is "a spiritual triumph beyond the wit of man;"
if "you are first made loyal through the power of some
one else who is loyal"; if "no social will can make the
community lovable unless loyalty is previously effective"; then the origin of "the beloved community" is
the great problem in the history of Christianity, and
everything points to Jesus as the only solution. He performed the miracle of the origin of life. A proper evalu-
ation of Jesus as the initiator would have been the natural
and necessary consummation of this entire doctrine of
salvation by loyalty.

A tacit condition is attached to all the high claims made by Professor Royce and others on behalf of the Church: If the Church is to have saving power, it must embody Christ. He is the revolutionary force within it. The saving qualities of the Church depend on the question whether it has translated the personal life of Jesus Christ into the social life of its group and thus brings it to bear on the individual. If Christ is not in the Church, how does it differ from " the world "? It will still assimilate its members, but it will not make them persons bearing the family likeness of the first-born son of God.

Wherever the Church has lost the saving influence of Christ, it has lost its saltness and is a tasteless historical survival. Therewith all theological doctrines about it become untrue. Antiquity and continuity are no substitute for the vitality of the Christ-spirit. Age, instead of being a presumption in favor of a religious body, is a question-mark set over against its name. The world is full of stale religion. It is historically self-evident that church bodies do lose the saving power. In fact, they may become social agencies to keep their people stupid, stationary, superstitious, bigoted, and ready to choke their first-born ideals and instincts as a sacrifice to the God of stationariness whom their religious guides have imposed on them. Wherever an aged and proud Church sets up high claims as an indispensable institution of salvation, let it be tested by the cleanliness, education, and moral elasticity of the agricultural labourers whom it has long controlled, or of the slum dwellers who have long ago slipped out of its control.

This conditional form of predicating the saving power
and spiritual authority of the Church is only one more
way of asserting that in anything which claims to be
Christian, religion must have an immediate ethical nexus
and effect. This marks an essential difference between
the claims made for the Church in Catholic theology,
and the emphasis on the functions of the Church made
in the social gospel. The Catholic doctrine of the Church
made its holiness, its power to forgive sin, and the effi-
cacy of its sacraments independent of the moral character of its priests and people ; the social conception makes
everything conditional on the spiritual virtues of the
church group. The Catholic conception stakes the claims
of the Church and its clergy on the due legal succession
and canonical ordination of its chief officers. This imports legal conceptions derived from the imperial Roman
bureaucracy into the organism of the Christian Church,
which has nothing to do with any bureaucracy. It gives
an unquestioned status to some corrupt, venal, or ignorant
bishop in Southern Italy ; makes the ecclesiastical validity
of the entire Anglican clergy dubious; and denies all
standing to Chalmers, Spurgeon, or Asbury. The social
gospel, on the other hand, tests the claims and powers
of any Church by the continuity of the apostolic faith
within it and by its possession of the law and spirit of
Jesus.

The saving power of the Church does not rest on its
institutional character, on its continuity, its ordination,
its ministry, or its doctrine. It rests on the presence of
the Kingdom of God within her. The Church grows

old; the Kingdom is ever young. The Church is a perpetuation of the past; the Kingdom is the power of the coming age. Unless the Church is vitalized by the ever nascent forces of the Kingdom within her, she deadens instead of begetting.

CHAPTER XIII

THE KINGDOM OF GOD

IF theology is to offer an adequate doctrinal basis for the social gospel, it must not only make room for the doctrine of the Kingdom of God, but give it a central place and revise all other doctrines so that they will articulate organically with it.

This doctrine is itself the social gospel. Without it, the idea of redeeming the social order will be but an annex to the orthodox conception of the scheme of salvation. It will live like a negro servant family in a detached cabin back of the white man's house in the South. If this doctrine gets the place which has always been its legitimate right, the practical proclamation and application of social morality will have a firm footing.

To those whose minds live in the social gospel, the Kingdom of God is a dear truth, the marrow of the gospel, just as the incarnation was to Athanasius, justification by faith alone to Luther, and the sovereignty of God to Jonathan Edwards. It was just as dear to Jesus. He too lived in it, and from it looked out on the world and the work he had to do.

Jesus always spoke of the Kingdom of God. Only two of his reported sayings contain the word "Church," and both passages are of questionable authenticity. It is safe to say that he never thought of founding the kind

131

of institution which afterward claimed to be acting for him. Yet immediately after his death, groups of disciples joined and consolidated by inward necessity. Each local group knew that it was part of a divinely founded fellowship mysteriously spreading through humanity, and awaiting the return of the Lord and the establishing of his Kingdom. This universal Church was loved with the same religious faith and reverence with which Jesus had loved the Kingdom of God. It was the partial and earthly realization of the divine Society, and at the Parousia the Church and the Kingdom would merge.

But the Kingdom was merely a hope, the Church a present reality. The chief interest and affection flowed toward the Church. Soon, through a combination of causes, the name and idea of " the Kingdom " began to be displaced by the name and idea of " the Church " in the preaching, literature, and theological thought of the Church. Augustine completed this process in his *De Civitate Dei*. The Kingdom of God which has, throughout human history, opposed the Kingdom of Sin, is to-day embodied in the Church. The millennium began when the Church was founded. This practically substituted the actual, not the ideal Church for the Kingdom of God. The beloved ideal of Jesus became a vague phrase which kept intruding from the New Testament. Like Cinderella in the kitchen, it saw the other great dogmas furbished up for the ball, but no prince of theology restored it to its rightful place. The Reformation, too, brought no renascence of the doctrine of the Kingdom; it had only eschatological value, or was defined in blurred phrases borrowed from the Church. The present revival of the Kingdom idea is due to the combined influence of the historical study of the Bible and of the social gospel.

When the doctrine of the Kingdom of God shriveled to an undeveloped and pathetic remnant in Christian thought, this loss was bound to have far-reaching consequences. We are told that the loss of a single tooth from the arch of the mouth in childhood may spoil the symmetrical development of the skull and produce malformations affecting the mind and character. The atrophy of that idea which had occupied the chief place in the mind of Jesus, necessarily affected the conception of Christianity, the life of the Church, the progress of humanity, and the structure of theology. I shall briefly enumerate some of the consequences affecting theology. This list, however, is by no means complete.

1. Theology lost its contact with the synoptic thought of Jesus. Its problems were not at all the same which had occupied his mind. It lost his point of view and became to some extent incapable of understanding him. His ideas had to be rediscovered in our time. Traditional theology and the mind of Jesus Christ became incommensurable quantities. It claimed to regard his revelation and the substance of his thought as divine, and yet did not learn to think like him. The loss of the Kingdom idea is one key to this situation.

2. The distinctive ethical principles of Jesus were the direct outgrowth of his conception of the Kingdom of God. When the latter disappeared from theology, the

former disappeared from ethics. Only persons having
the substance of the Kingdom ideal in their minds, seem
to be able to get relish out of the ethics of Jesus. Only
those church bodies which have been in opposition to
organized society and have looked for a better city
with its foundations in heaven, have taken the Sermon
on the Mount seriously.

3. The Church is primarily a fellowship for worship;
the Kingdom is a fellowship of righteousness. When
the latter was neglected in theology, the ethical force of
Christianity was weakened; when the former was emphasized in theology, the importance of worship was exaggerated. The prophets and Jesus had cried down sacrifices and ceremonial performances, and cried up righteousness, mercy, solidarity. Theology now reversed
this, and by its theoretical discussions did its best to
stimulate sacramental actions and priestly importance.
Thus the religious energy and enthusiasm which might
have saved mankind from its great sins, were used up in
hearing and endowing masses, or in maintaining competitive church organizations, while mankind is still stuck in
the mud. There are nations in which the ethical condition of the masses is the reverse of the frequency of the
masses in the churches.

4. When the Kingdom ceased to be the dominating
religious reality, the Church moved up into the position
of the supreme good. To promote the power of the
Church and its control over all rival political forces was
equivalent to promoting the supreme ends of Christianity. This increased the arrogance of churchmen and
took the moral check off their policies. For the King-

dom of God can never be promoted by lies, craft, crime or war, but the wealth and power of the Church have often been promoted by these means. The medieval ideal of the supremacy of the Church over the State was the logical consequence of making the Church the highest good with no superior ethical standard by which to test it. The medieval doctrines concerning the Church and the Papacy were the direct theological outcome of the struggles for Church supremacy, and were meant to be weapons in that struggle.

5. The Kingdom ideal is the test and corrective of the influence of the Church. When the Kingdom ideal disappeared, the conscience of the Church was muffled. It became possible for the missionary expansion of Christianity to halt for centuries without creating any sense of shortcoming. It became possible for the most unjust social conditions to fasten themselves on Christian nations without awakening any consciousness that the purpose of Christ was being defied and beaten back. The practical undertakings of the Church remained within narrow lines, and the theological thought of the Church was necessarily confined in a similar way. The claims of the Church were allowed to stand in theology with no conditions and obligations to test and balance them. If the Kingdom had stood as the purpose for which the Church exists, the Church could not have fallen into such corruption and sloth. Theology bears part of the guilt for the pride, the greed, and the ambition of the Church.

6. The Kingdom ideal contains the revolutionary force of Christianity. When this ideal faded out of

the systematic thought of the Church, it became a conservative social influence and increased the weight of the other stationary forces in society. If the Kingdom of God had remained part of the theological and Christian consciousness, the Church could not, down to our times, have been salaried by autocratic class governments to keep the democratic and economic impulses of the people under check.

7. Reversely, the movements for democracy and social justice were left without a religious backing for lack of the Kingdom idea. The Kingdom of God as the fellowship of righteousness, would be advanced by the abolition of industrial slavery and the disappearance of the slums of civilization; the Church would only indirectly gain through such social changes. Even today many Christians can not see any religious importance in social justice and fraternity because it does not increase the number of conversions nor fill the churches. Thus the practical conception of salvation, which is the effective theology of the common man and minister, has been cut back and crippled for lack of the Kingdom ideal.

8. Secular life is belittled as compared with church life. Services rendered to the Church get a higher religious rating than services rendered to the community.[1] Thus the religious value is taken out of the activities of the common man and the prophetic services to society. Wherever the Kingdom of God is a living reality in

[1] After the death of Susan B. Anthony a minister commented on her life, regretting that she was not orthodox in her beliefs. In the same address he spoke glowingly about a new linoleum laid in the church kitchen.

Christian thought, any advance of social righteousness is seen as a part of redemption and arouses inward joy and the triumphant sense of salvation. When the Church absorbs interest, a subtle asceticism creeps back into our theology and the world looks different.

9. When the doctrine of the Kingdom of God is lacking in theology, the salvation of the individual is seen in its relation to the Church and to the future life, but not in its relation to the task of saving the social order. Theology has left this important point in a condition so hazy and muddled that it has taken us almost a generation to see that the salvation of the individual and the redemption of the social order are closely related, and how.

10. Finally, theology has been deprived of the inspiration of great ideas contained in the idea of the Kingdom and in labor for it. The Kingdom of God breeds prophets; the Church breeds priests and theologians. The Church runs to tradition and dogma; the Kingdom of God rejoices in forecasts and boundless horizons. The men who have contributed the most fruitful impulses to Christian thought have been men of prophetic vision, and their theology has proved most effective for future times where it has been most concerned with past history, with present social problems, and with the future of human society. The Kingdom of God is to theology what outdoor colour and light are to art. It is impossible to estimate what inspirational impulses have been lost to theology and to the Church, because it did not develop the doctrine of the Kingdom of God and see the world and its redemption from that point of view.

These are some of the historical effects which the
loss of the doctrine of the Kingdom of God has inflicted
on systematic theology. The chief contribution which
the social gospel has made and will make to theology is
to give new vitality and importance to that doctrine. In
doing so it will be a reformatory force of the highest importance in the field of doctrinal theology, for any systematic conception of Christianity must be not only
defective but incorrect if the idea of the Kingdom of
God does not govern it.

The restoration of the doctrine of the Kingdom has
already made progress. Some of the ablest and most
voluminous works of the old theology in their thousands
of pages gave the Kingdom of God but a scanty mention, usually in connection with eschatology, and saw no
connection between it and the Calvinistic doctrines of
personal redemption. The newer manuals not only make
constant reference to it in connection with various doctrines, but they arrange their entire subject matter so
that the Kingdom of God becomes the governing idea. [1]

---

[1] William Adams Brown, "Christian Theology in Outline," p. 192:
"We are witnessing to-day a reaction against this exaggerated
individualism (of Reformation theology). It has become an axiom
of modern thought that the government of God has social as well
as individual significance, and the conception of the Kingdom of
God — obscured in the earlier Protestantism — is coming again
into the forefront of theological thought." See the discussion on
"The View of the Kingdom in Modern Thought" which follows.
    Albrecht Ritschl, in his great monograph on Justification and
Reconciliation, begins the discussion of his own views in Volume
III (§ 2) by insisting that personal salvation .must be organically
connected with the Kingdom of God. He says ("Rechtfertigung
und Versöhnung," III, p. 111): "Theology has taken a very un-
equal interest in the two chief characteristics of Christianity.
Everything pertaining to its character as the redemption of men

In the following brief propositions I should like to offer a few suggestions, on behalf of the social gospel, for the theological formulation of the doctrine of the Kingdom. Something like this is needed to give us "a theology for the social gospel."

1. The Kingdom of God is divine in its origin, progress and consummation. It was initiated by Jesus Christ, in whom the prophetic spirit came to its consummation, it is sustained by the Holy Spirit, and it will be brought to its fulfilment by the power of God in his own time. The passive and active resistance of the Kingdom of Evil at every stage of its advance is so great, and the human resources of the Kingdom of God so slender, that no explanation can satisfy a religious mind which does not see the power of God in its movements. The Kingdom of God, therefore, is miraculous all the way, and is the continuous revelation of the power, the righteousness, and the love of God. The establishment of a community of

has been made the subject of the most minute consideration; consequently redemption by Christ has been taken as the centre of all Christian knowledge and life, whereas the ethical conception of Christianity contained in the idea of the Kingdom of God has been slighted. . . . It has been fatal for Protestantism that the Reformers did not cleanse the idea of the ethical Kingdom of God or Christ from its hierarchical corruption (i. e. the idea that the visible Church is identical with the Kingdom), but worked out the idea only in an academic and unpractical form." Kant first recognized the importance of the Kingdom of God for ethics. Schleiermacher first applied the teleological quality of Christianity to the definition of its nature, but he still treated now of personal redemption and now of the Kingdom of God, without adequately working out their connection. Ritschl has done more than any one else to put the idea to the front in German theology, but he does not get beyond a few great general ideas. He was born too early to get sociological ideas.

righteousness in mankind is just as much a saving act of God as the salvation of an individual from his natural selfishness and moral inability. The Kingdom of God, therefore, is not merely ethical, but has a rightful place in theology. This doctrine is absolutely necessary to establish that organic union between religion and morality, between theology and ethics, which is one of the characteristics of the Christian religion. When our moral actions are consciously related to the Kingdom of God they gain religious quality. Without this doctrine we shall have expositions of schemes of redemption and we shall have systems of ethics, but we shall not have a true exposition of Christianity. The first step to the reform of the Churches is the restoration of the doctrine of the Kingdom of God.

2. The Kingdom of God contains the teleology of the Christian religion. It translates theology from the static to the dynamic. It sees, not doctrines or rites to be conserved and perpetuated, but resistance to be overcome and great ends to be achieved. Since the Kingdom of God is the supreme purpose of God, we shall understand the Kingdom so far as we understand God, and we shall understand God so far as we understand his Kingdom. As long as organized sin is in the world, the Kingdom of God is characterized by conflict with evil. But if there were no evil, or after evil has been overcome, the Kingdom of God will still be the end to which God is lifting the race. It is realized not only by redemption, but also by the education of mankind and the revelation of his life within it.

3. Since God is in it, the Kingdom of God is always

both present and future. Like God it is in all tenses, eternal in the midst of time. It is the energy of God realizing itself in human life. Its future lies among the mysteries of God. It invites and justifies prophecy, but all prophecy is fallible; it is valuable in so far as it grows out of action for the Kingdom and impels action. No theories about the future of the Kingdom of God are likely to be valuable or true which paralyze or postpone redemptive action on our part. To those who postpone, it is a theory and not a reality. It is for us to see the Kingdom of God as always coming, always pressing in on the present, always big with possibility, and always inviting immediate action. We walk by faith. Every human life is so placed that it can share with God in the creation of the Kingdom, or can resist and retard its progress. The Kingdom is for each of us the supreme task and the supreme gift of God. By accepting it as a task, we experience it as a gift. By labouring for it we enter into the joy and peace of the Kingdom as our divine fatherland and habitation.

4. Even before Christ, men of God saw the Kingdom of God as the great end to which all divine leadings were pointing. Every idealistic interpretation of the world, religious or philosophical, needs some such conception. Within the Christian religion the idea of the Kingdom gets its distinctive interpretation from Christ. (a) Jesus emancipated the idea of the Kingdom from previous nationalistic limitations and from the debasement of lower religious tendencies, and made it world-wide and spiritual. (b) He made the purpose of salvation essential in it. (c) He imposed his own mind, his personality,

his love and holy will on the idea of the Kingdom. (d)
He not only foretold it but initiated it by his life and
work. As humanity more and more develops a racial
consciousness in modern life, idealistic interpretations of
the destiny of humanity will become more influential and
important. Unless theology has a solidaristic vision
higher and fuller than any other, it can not maintain the
spiritual leadership of mankind, but will be outdistanced.
Its business is to infuse the distinctive qualities of Jesus
Christ into its teachings about the Kingdom, and this will
be a fresh competitive test of his continued headship of
humanity.

5. The Kingdom of God is humanity organized according to the will of God. Interpreting it through the consciousness of Jesus we may affirm these convictions about
the ethical relations within the Kingdom: (a) Since
Christ revealed the divine worth of life and personality,
and since his salvation seeks the restoration and fulfilment of even the least, it follows that the Kingdom of
God, at every stage of human development, tends toward
a social order which will best guarantee to all personalities their freest and highest development. This involves
the redemption of social life from the cramping influence
of religious bigotry, from the repression of self-assertion
in the relation of upper and lower classes, and from all
forms of slavery in which human beings are treated as
mere means to serve the ends of others. (b) Since love
is the supreme law of Christ, the Kingdom of God im-
plies a progressive reign of love in human affairs. We
can see its advance wherever the free will of love super-
sedes the use of force and legal coercion as a regulative of

the social order. This involves the redemption of society from political autocracies and economic oligarchies; the substitution of redemptive for vindictive penology; the abolition of constraint through hunger as part of the industrial system; and the abolition of war as the supreme expression of hate and the completest cessation of freedom. (c) The highest expression of love is the free surrender of what is truly our own, life, property, and rights. A much lower but perhaps more decisive expression of love is the surrender of any opportunity to exploit men. No social group or organization can claim to be clearly within the Kingdom of God which drains others for its own ease, and resists the effort to abate this fundamental evil. This involves the redemption of society from private property in the natural resources of the earth, and from any condition in industry which makes monopoly profits possible. (d) The reign of love tends toward the progressive unity of mankind, but with the maintenance of individual liberty and the opportunity of nations to work out their own national peculiarities and ideals.

6. Since the Kingdom is the supreme end of God, it must be the purpose for which the Church exists. The measure in which it fulfils this purpose is also the measure of its spiritual authority and honour. The institutions of the Church, its activities, its worship, and its theology must in the long run be tested by its effectiveness in creating the Kingdom of God. For the Church to see itself apart from the Kingdom, and to find its aims in itself, is the same sin of selfish detachment as when an individual selfishly separates himself from the com-

mon good. The Church has the power to save in so far
as the Kingdom of God is present in it. If the Church is
not living for the Kingdom, its institutions are part of
the " world." In that case it is not the power of redemption but its object. It may even become an anti-Christian
power. If any form of church organization which formerly aided the Kingdom now impedes it, the reason for
its existence is gone.

7. Since the Kingdom is the supreme end, all problems
of personal salvation must be reconsidered from the
point of view of the Kingdom. It is not sufficient to set
the two aims of Christianity side by side. There must
be a synthesis, and theology must explain how the two
react on each other. (See Chapter X of this book.)
The entire redemptive work of Christ must also be reconsidered under this orientation. Early Greek theology
saw salvation chiefly as the redemption from ignorance by
the revelation of God and from earthliness by the impartation of immortality. It interpreted the work of
Christ accordingly, and laid stress on his incarnation and
resurrection. Western theology saw salvation mainly
as forgiveness of guilt and freedom from punishment.
It interpreted the work of Christ accordingly, and laid
stress on the death and atonement. If the Kingdom of
God was the guiding idea and chief end of Jesus — as
we now know it was — we may be sure that every step
in His life, including His death, was related to that aim
and its realization, and when the idea of the Kingdom of
God takes its due place in theology, the work of Christ
will have to be interpreted afresh.

8. The Kingdom of God is not confined within the

limits of the Church and its activities. It embraces the whole of human life. It is the Christian transfiguration of the social order. The Church is one social institution alongside of the family, the industrial organization of society, and the State. The Kingdom of God is in all these, and realizes itself through them all. During the Middle Ages all society was ruled and guided by the Church. Few of us would want modern life to return to such a condition. Functions which the Church used to perform, have now far outgrown its capacities. The Church is indispensable to the religious education of humanity and to the conservation of religion, but the greatest future awaits religion in the public life of humanity.

CHAPTER XIV

THE INITIATOR OF THE KINGDOM OF GOD

THE social gospel has an inherent interest in history. Individualistic theology sees everywhere countless sinful individuals who must all go through the same process of repentance, faith, justification, and regeneration, and who in due time die and go to heaven or hell. The historical age in which a person lived, or the social class or race to which he belonged, matters little. This religious point of view is above time and history. On the other hand the social gospel tries to see the progress of the Kingdom of God in the flow of history; not only in the doings of the Church, but in the clash of economic forces and social classes, in the rise and fall of despotisms and forms of enslavement, in the rise of new value-judgments and fresh canons of moral taste and sentiment, or the elevation or decline of moral standards. Its chief interest is the Kingdom of God; and the Kingdom of God is history seen in a religious and teleological way. Therefore the social gospel is always historically minded. Its spread goes hand in hand with the spread of the historical spirit and method.

This dominant interest in the creation and progress of social redemption influences the approach to the theological problems of the person and work of Christ. We

want to see the Christ who initiated the Kingdom of
God.   Theologians have always tried to make their
christology match with their conception of salvation.
If they believed salvation to consist chiefly in the knowledge of God, they emphasized the personality and the
doctrine of Christ as the complete revelation of God.
If they made salvation to consist chiefly in the mystic
impartation of divine life and immortality, their christology laid chief stress on the union of the divine and
human in the incarnation and in the sacraments.   If salvation consists above all in the expiation of guilt, the
forgiveness of sins, the justification of the sinner, and the
remission of his penalties, then we need a Christ who
made atonement for our sins, rendered satisfaction to
God for our delinquencies, and offset our guilty defects
by his infinite merit and divine virtue.   Each conception of salvation made a pragmatic selection and construction of the facts.   Each was fragmentary, but without necessarily excluding other series of ideas.   So now
the social gospel, without excluding other theological convictions, demands to understand that Christ who set in
motion the historical forces of redemption which are
to overthrow the Kingdom of Evil.

This is surely not an illegitimate interest.   It is a return to the earliest messianic theology; whereas some
of the other christological interests and ideas are alien
importations, part of that wave of " Hellenization "
which nearly swamped the original gospel.

Being historically minded and realistic in its interests,
the social gospel is less concerned in the metaphysical
problems involved in the trinitarian and christological

doctrines. The speculative problem of christological dogma was how the divine and human natures united in the one person of Christ; the problem of the social gospel is how the divine life of Christ can get control of human society. The social gospel is concerned about a progressive social incarnation of God.

The social gospel is believed by trinitarians and unitarians alike, by Catholic Modernists and Kansas Presbyterians of the most cerulean colour. It arouses a fresh and warm loyalty to Christ wherever it goes, though not always a loyalty to the Church. All who believe in it are at one in desiring the spiritual sovereignty of Christ in humanity. Their attitude to the problems of the creeds will usually be determined by other influences.

Yet there are certain qualities in the social gospel which may create a feeling of apathy toward the speculative questions. It is modern and is out for realities. It is ethical and wants ethical results from theology. It is solidaristic and feels homesick in the atomistic desert of individualism.

The social gospel joins with all modern thought in the feeling that the old theology does not give us a Christ who is truly personal. Just as the human race, when it appears in theology, is an amorphous metaphysical conception which could be more briefly designated by an algebraic symbol, in the same way the personality of Jesus is not allowed to be real under theological influence. If it does stand out vital and resolute, it is in spite of theology and not because of it. Some of the

the personal Christ gives us the social gospel

greatest theologians, men who wrote epoch-making treatises about Christ, such as Athanasius, give no indication that the personality of Jesus was live and real to them. When those who have been trained under the old religious beliefs come under the influence of historical teaching, the realization that Jesus was actually a person, and not merely part of a " scheme of redemption," often comes as a great and beneficent shock. He has been made part of a scheme of salvation, the second premise in a great syllogism. The social gospel wants to see a personality able to win hearts, dominate situations, able to bind men in loyalty and make them think like himself, and to set revolutionary social forces in motion.

[margin note: Weber's charismatic leader!]

Every event and saying in the life of Christ has, of course, been scanned intensely and used over and over for edification or theological proof. But in the main the theological significance of the life of Christ has been comprised in the incarnation, the atonement, and the resurrection. The life in general served mainly to connect and lead up to these great events, and to found the Church.[1] The things in which Jesus himself was passionately interested and which he strove to accomplish, do not seem to count for much. The impartation of divine life and immortality to the race was accomplished when he was a babe. The atonement might actually have been frustrated if the life effort of Jesus had been

---

[1] The treatment of his " work " under the three heads of prophet, priest, and king, which is an hereditary scheme in theology, seems antique and far-fetched. Moreover, his kingly office mainly begins with his resurrection. His kingly work in historical life has been treated with neglect.

successful, for if the Jews had accepted his spiritual leadership, they would not have killed him.

The social gospel would interpret all the events of his life, including his death, by the dominant purpose which he consistently followed, the establishment of the Kingdom of God. This is the only interpretation which would have appealed to himself. His life was what counted; his death was part of it. The historic current of salvation which went out from him is the prolongation of that life into which he put his conscious energy. Theology has made the divinity of Christ a question of nature rather than character. His divinity was an inheritance or endowment which he brought with him and which was fixed for him in his pre-existent state. He was divine on account of what took place at one moment in the womb of one Jewish woman rather than on account of all that took place in the inner depths of his spirit when he communed with his Father and fought through the issues of his life. Theology has been on a false trail in seeking the key to his life in the difficult doctrine of the two natures. That doctrine has never been settled. The formula of Chalcedon was a compromise. Any attempt to think precisely about the question results in a caricature; safety lies in vagueness. We shall come closer to the secret of Jesus if we think less of the physical process of conception and more of the spiritual processes of desire, choice, affirmation, and self-surrender within his own will and personality. The mysteries of the spiritual world take place within the will.

To repeat: The social gospel is not primarily interested in metaphysical questions; its christological interest is all for a real personality who could set a great historical process in motion; it wants his work interpreted by the purposes which ruled and directed his active life; it would have more interest in basing the divine quality of his personality on free and ethical acts of his will than in dwelling on the passive inheritance of a divine essence.

The fundamental first step in the salvation of mankind was the achievement of the personality of Jesus. Within him the Kingdom of God got its first foothold in humanity. It was by virtue of his personality that he became the initiator of the Kingdom.

His personality was an achievement, not an effortless inheritance. His temptations and struggles were not stage-combats. At every point of his life he had to see his way through the tangle of moral questions which invited to errors and misjudgments; his clarity of judgment was an achievement. Not only in the desert but all the way he had to re-affirm his unity with the will of God and make all aims subservient to the Kingdom of God. The inclination early set in to eliminate the element of temptation, of effort, of vigorous action and reaction, and to show him calm, majestic, omniscient, the effortless master of all forces. This was supposed to be the proper demonstration of divinity in human form; in fact it was a demonstration of feeble imagination and of Gnostic tendencies in his interpreters. Possibly God might be revealed in a life wholly placid and complete; certainly the Kingdom of God could not be initiated by such a life, for the Kingdom of God means battle. In

issue of the nec. role resistance plays # in revelation?

all other cases we judge the ethical worth of a man by the character he achieves by will and effort. If he has any unusual outfit of nature we deduct it in our estimate. How can we claim high ethical value for the personality and character of Jesus if no effort of will was necessary to achieve it?

Jesus lived out his own life. Like every other Ego he existed for himself as well as for others. He was asserting and defending his right to be himself when he stood up for others. The problems of human life were not simply official problems to him, but personal problems. But unlike others, he did not fall into the sin of selfishness, because he succeeded in uniting the service of the common good with the affirmation of his selfhood.

The personality which he achieved was a new type in humanity. Having the power to master and assimilate others, it became the primal cell of a new social organism. Even if there had been no sin from which mankind had to be redeemed, the life of Jesus would have dated an epoch in the evolution of the race by the introduction of a new type and consequently new social standards. He is the real revelation of God. Other conceptions have to be outlived; his has to be attained.

In the words of one of the most personal and original idealistic philosophers: "The consciousness of the absolute unity of the human and the divine life is the profoundest insight possible to man. Before Jesus it did not exist. Since his time, we might say to this day, it has been almost lost again, at least in secular philosophy. Jesus evidently had this insight. How did he get it? There is nothing very wonderful in rediscovering the truth after another man has found the way; but how the first, separated by ages before and after by the sole possession of this insight, obtained it, this is matter for profound wonder. Therefore it is really true that Jesus of Nazareth, in a unique way, true of no other, is the only begotten and first born Son of God, and that all ages, if they are capable of understanding him at all, must recognize him as such. It is true enough that now any man can rediscover this doctrine in the writings of the apostles and appropriate it in his own convictions. It is also true, and we assert it, that the philosopher,— as far as he knows,— discovers the same truths independently of Christianity, and sees them with a clearness and breadth of vision which traditional Christianity can not match. Yet it remains for ever true that we, our entire age, and all our philosophical investigations are based on Christianity, and our thinking proceeds from it; that this Christian faith has entered in the most manifold ways into our entire culture; and that we all would not be what we are, unless this powerful principle had preceded us historically. It remains incontestably true that all those who since Jesus have arrived at union with God, have attained it only through him and by his mediation. Thus in every way it is confirmed that to the end of time all wise men will bow before this Jesus of Nazareth, and the more of life they have themselves, the more humbly will they acknowledge the exceeding glory of this great personality." [1]

[1] Johann Gottlieb Fichte, "Die Anweisung zum seligen Leben," Lecture VI. 1806. The translation is mine.

The essentializing
the unique newness.

Jesus experienced God in a new way. The ethical monotheism which he inherited from the prophets was transformed within his spirit and through his experiences into something far lovelier and kinder. Jehovah, the keeper of covenants and judge of his people, was changed into the Father in heaven who forgives sins freely, welcomes the prodigal, makes his sun to shine on the just and unjust, and asks for nothing but love, trust, and cooperative obedience. This intuition of God was born in a life that neither hated nor feared, and so far as it is adopted in any single life or in the life of humanity, it banishes hate and fear. An overpowering consciousness of God is needed in order to offset and overcome the tyranny of the sensuous life and its temptations. This consciousness of God which we derive from Jesus is able to establish centres of spiritual strength and peace which help to break the free sweep of evil in social life. Jesus set love into the centre of the spiritual universe, and all life is illuminated from that centre. This is the highest idealistic faith ever conceived, and the greatest addition ever made to the spiritual possessions of mankind.

With such a Father spiritual intimacy is possible. With a despotic God prayer is a series of court obeisances and a secret fencing for personal independence. But given such a God as Jesus knew, and the consciousness of him would steal in everywhere and envelop all life in peace. It made righteousness a joy and sin repulsive. Any one who has ever been under a clear and happy realization of God will remember how spontaneous goodness becomes.

So we have in Jesus a perfect religious personality,

a spiritual life completely filled by the realization of a God who is love. All his mind was set on God and one with him. Consequently it was also absorbed in the fundamental purpose of God, the Kingdom of God. Like the idea of God, the conception of the Kingdom was both an inheritance and a creation of Jesus; he received it and transformed it in accordance with his consciousness of God. Within his mind the punitive and imperialistic elements were steeped out of it, and the elements of love and solidarity were dyed into it. The Reign of God came to mean the organized fellowship of humanity acting under the impulse of love.

By virtue of this consciousness of God Jesus rose above three temptations which have beset other religious spirits.

The first temptation is mysticism. Those who have been initiated into the secret inner way of God, and have experienced the sweetness of losing self in the all-comprehending and holy Life, are tempted to turn in high disdain from the small and material contacts and duties which bind the soul on the wheel that ever revolves and never gets anywhere, and to seek the tranquillity and forgetfulness of mystic absorption. This is one of the temptations of the noblest souls.

Jesus was not a mystic in the narrower sense of the escape from the world. He is our great example of prayer and of intimate communion with God. But the Kingdom of God engaged his will and set his task in the midst of men. He drew his strength from God, but he put it forth in the world. The Kingdom of God put di-

vine significance into all his minor duties and saved
life from religious disdain. We all know the common
statue of Buddha, with his hands relaxed and inactive
in his lap, his eyes unseeing and visionary, his lips in
the smile of mystic contentment. We can not see Jesus
so.

The second temptation is pessimism. Religion creates a profound sense of the evil in life. Those whose
ears are attuned to hear the deepest organ note of the
universe, hear a groan of travail from the under deep.
Consequently pessimism has been the sombre habitation
of many noble religious minds from Buddha to Schopen-
hauer. The dualism of the first century, both philosophical and religious, was an expression of pessimism.
Christianity was sucked thigh-deep into this quicksand.
Its earliest speculative theologians, the Gnostics, were so
pessimistic that to them the creation of the world was a
blunder or a crime, and the Creator-God of Judaism got
no reverence from them for perpetrating this world.

Jesus was not a pessimist. Since God was love, this
world was to him fundamentally good. He realized not
only evil but the Kingdom of Evil; but he launched
the Kingdom of God against it, and staked his life on its
triumph. His faith in God and in the Kingdom of God
constituted him a religious optimist. Even when his life
was overshadowed by opposition, seeming failure, and
death, his prevailing temper was not melancholy, but
youthful and triumphant. He had no use for the studied
melancholy of periodical fasting. Why should his
friends fast? They were having a wedding time. Why
pour the new wine of gladness into the old sad bottles,

and why sew a new patch on a garment that was dropping
to pieces?

The third temptation of religious spirits is asceticism
and other-worldliness. Both are related to pessimism.
The monk repudiates the social life which tempts him,
scours the stains of worldliness from his soul by spiritual exercises, wears the earthly integument thin by
hunger and castigation, and enjoys the other world by
anticipation whenever angels visit him or he has a vision
of divine glory. All Christians who yearn to escape
from this vale of tears and whose life is really set on another world, are to that extent pessimistic. The asceticism and other-worldliness of ancient and mediaeval
Christianity were results of its " Hellenization," as Harnack calls it. It took a thousand years of history, great
social and intellectual changes, and an unparalleled religious revolution to set Christianity even partly free from
these influences of its early Greek and Oriental environment.

Jesus was neither ascetic nor other-worldly. He formulated the distinctive difference between himself and
John the Baptist in the saying that John ate not and
drank not, while he himself ate and drank, and quoted
the critics who called him a glutton and wine-bibber.
He believed in a life after death, but it was not the dominant element in his teaching, nor the constraining force
in his religious life. There are sayings in the gospels
which are ascetic, and more that are apocalyptic; but
Jesus, I believe, was neither. In so far as these sayings
were really his own, their ideas were part of the equipment furnished him by his age and religion; they were

not the essential products of his life. His mind was
not at all of the same family type as those who wrote
and re-wrote the apocalyptic literature. He fasted when
he was absorbed in thought; so did Socrates; so do
others. He went without food, sleep, and home-life because he was set on a big thing. This is the revolutionary asceticism of the Kingdom of God, but that is wholly
different from the individualistic and other-worldly asceticism of the Nitrian desert.

My own conviction is that the professional theologians
of Europe, who all belong by kinship and sympathy to
the bourgeois classes and are constitutionally incapaci-
tated for understanding any revolutionary ideas, past or
present, have overemphasized the ascetic and eschatological elements in the teachings of Jesus. They have
classed as ascetic or apocalyptic the radical sayings about
property and non-resistance which seem to them unpractical or visionary. If the present chastisement of God
purges our intellects of capitalistic and upper-class iniquities, we shall no longer damn these sayings by calling
them eschatological, but shall exhibit them as anticipa-
tions of the fraternal ethics of democracy and prophecies
of social common sense.

Jesus communed with God; he realized the evil in the
world; and he held his life with a light grasp. Yet he
escaped the noble temptations of religion contained in
mysticism, pessimism, asceticism, and other-worldliness.
Out of the same ingredients, communion with God,
realization of evil, and religious intensity and self-control, he built a higher synthesis. His attitude to life was
the direct product of his twofold belief, in the Father

who is love and the Kingdom of God which is righteousness.   Mediaeval Christianity, which was mystic, ascetic, and other-worldly, was not built on his synthesis.
On the other hand the social gospel can be.   His affirmation of life is the ideal basis for the social gospel.   No
religion involving the negation of life is really compatible with it.   It remains to be seen whether anything like the social gospel can make headway in
Buddhistic countries; and if it does, whether it will
not transform the old Buddhism.

His communion with God and his devotion to the
Kingdom of God set Jesus free and also bound him.
They freed him from the conservatism of inherited religion and from the coercion of the social order; they
bound him to a life of obedience and to the utter service of men.   The harmony of these antinomies is one
of the distinctive qualities of his personality.

He was a loyal son of his nation, a believer in its
traditions and its worth, and we know how deeply he
was moved by his foresight of its disaster.   His religious
life was inseparable from that of his nation.   There were
no novel or alien elements in it, as with Paul or Philo,
which might have laid the basis for departures.   He
never cut loose from the religion of his fathers, and
never told his followers to leave the synagogue and
found the Church.   He was no come-outer.

But he had a higher law and allegiance within him.
In so far as the religious customs of Judaism conflicted
with his consciousness of God or with the reign of love,
he broke with them.   He contravened the Sabbath regu-

lations when they inflicted suffering or interfered with acts of mercy. He set aside the entire principle of clean and unclean food because it had no ethical truth in it. The Sermon on the Mount was a deliberate declaration that the old moral law was insufficient and that new ethical standards were needed for the new era. His invective against the scribes and Pharisees repudiated, not only the clerical " system " which was exploiting religion, but the models, definitions, and casuistry of current theology. Aside from his action of cleansing " the house of prayer " from the chatter of the market, he scarcely mentioned the temple and its sacrifices, except to rank them below love and reconciliation. Ceremonial acts were not the proper expression of his consciousness of God. He realized religion in acts expressing love and fellowship, or in breaking with the Kingdom of Evil. Under his teaching the burden of time, expense and routine through which religious men sought to appease God's anger or court his favour, dropped away. If God was love, why these doings? " The Gentiles think they shall be heard for their many-worded prayers; be not like them; your Father knows."

Such a change of attitude toward the ritual institutions of religion, when it has become common, has availed to purge the religion of whole nations of its non-ethical inheritances; it has reinforced the progressive elements of society by turning the energies of religion from the maintenance of conservative institutions to the support of movements for political emancipation and social justice. Such a change in religion inaugurates new eras in history.

Now, such changes, when they have happened, have
been due in part to a renaissance of this attitude of
Jesus.   In the case of the Protestant Reformation it was
mainly due to a revival of Paul's attitude of freedom over
against the Law.   But Paul's freedom was one of the
treasures which he derived from Christ.

With Jesus this spiritual attitude toward the religious
customs of his people was the consistent outworking of
his consciousness of God and of his conception of the
reign of God.   In making his stand on each of the points
which brought him into conflict, he was achieving his
own personality.

the new definition of God

The God whom Jesus bore within him was not the
God of one nation.   The reign of God which he meant
to establish was not a new imperialism with the chosen
people on the top of the pile.   The gospels show us Jesus
in the act of crossing the racial boundary lines and out-
growing nationalistic religion.   He recognized the religious qualities in a pagan; he foresaw that the Kingdom of God would cut across the old lines of division;
he held up the hyphenated and heretical Samaritan as
a model of humane kindness.   Every time a wider contact was offered him, he seized it with a sense of exulta-
tion, like the discoverer of a new continent.   That
world-wide consciousness of humanity, which is coming
to some in protest against the hideous disruption and
hatred of the War, was won by Jesus at less cost under
the tuition of God and the Kingdom ideal.

Jesus lived in a world of high thought and set his face
toward the greatest of all aims.   But he talked peace-

fully with simple people, and was impatient when his
friends did not want him annoyed by children. He was
valorous, fearless, an outdoor man, and an invincible
fighter. But he was so tender to the sick and so com-
radely with the poor that " Christlike " has remained
one of the aristocratic adjectives in our language, and
men like Saint Francis, who followed him and grew like
him, have stood out as the beloved souls, the rare flowers
of esoteric humanity.

He was a proud spirit who lived out his own life and
asserted himself against all the weight of authority,
against his king, against the supreme court of his nation,
against Moses, against professional theology and the lawyer caste, against the power of custom, against his home
community, against his own mother. But he had a
thirst for friendship, an unfailing insight into the subtler
motives and longings of men and women, a thrilling re-
sponsiveness to the emotions of masses of men, and an
unexampled sense of the sacredness of personality.

He bowed to law and order. He paid his taxes, and
advised others to do it. He sent a leper to the proper
officer to get his sanitary certificate. But he had no
spiritual awe for the exponents of the present social order. He challenged its moral basis. He dropped into
the silence of a passive resister when he faced a typical
court, and he was felt then and ever since as a force
against despotism.

The personality of Jesus is a call to the emancipation of our own personalities. He has multiplied free
souls. Every such soul counts in the progress of mankind. They are rare. They are most effective in the

redemption of society when they are free from the acrid qualities of rebellion. Those who have derived their spiritual freedom and their social spirit from Jesus are most likely to have the combination of freedom with love and gentleness. This ought to be the distinctive mark of Christ within the social movement. Is it true that Jesus has been experienced as a Liberator more frequently apart from theology than within it? If so, why?

To think out any one of these convictions, or to achieve any one of these harmonies, so that all life can become simple, whole-hearted, and divinely intelligible through its truth, is a great achievement for a life-time. Luther was one of the most dynamic personalities in history, one of the epoch-making religious minds. Yet it took him years of morbid struggle to emerge from the gloom of religious fear into Christian assurance, and to cut across the labyrinth of church methods by the short-cut of simple faith. And after achieving this discovery, he imposed his emancipating faith on others as a sovereign formula, and would not let others advance beyond the point he had reached. With Jesus these great inward convictions were not academic theory, but life and action. They were the reality on which he staked all. They were so much his own that he acted on them as a matter of course, with a self-possession which did not have to weigh and consider, but struck ahead, and struck right.

In the case of biological mutations the question is not only whether the new type is valuable, but also whether it will breed true and succeed in perpetuating itself against the competition of other types. Jesus not only achieved the kind of religious personality which we have tried to bring before our memory and imagination, but he succeeded in perpetuating his spirit. What was personal with him became social within the group of the disciples. His life became a collective and assimilating force and a current of historic tradition.

His disciples were human stuff, and all of them doubtless were thin conductors for the powerful current they had to convey. His Jewish friends were full of older ideas, and most of them seem to have sagged back toward conservative Judaism. Luke's narrative about Peter and Stephen, and Paul's profound trouble of mind about the Judaizing brethren are evidence. As soon as the Church moved out into the Greek world, a process of assimilation began which left little of the real Jesus in sight. The historical research of the last forty years has written a new chapter about the sufferings of Jesus. Imagine him coming into a Gnostic conventicle in A. D. 150, or into the Church of Cyprian in A. D. 250, or into high mass at the Church of the Lateran in A. D. 1250, and trying to discover what it was all about.

And yet he survived. He has come through to this day with his thought and his personality still vital, *sui generis*, and far ahead of our day. Whenever his spirit has been embodied again in a striking degree in some individual, people have gathered around that man, hungry for salvation. Any man in whom the Jesus-strain reappears clearly is felt to be a kind of superman. If Tolstoi, for instance, had never begun to follow Christ in his life, he would be simply one of a group of brilliant Russian novelists. Since he received something of the mind of Jesus into his mind, he became one of the prophetic figures of our age and no one can tell how much he contributed, through others, to enable Russia, newly free, to make the one sincere and penetrating utterance made on behalf of democracy and peace in the Spring and Summer of 1917. In the same way those religious movements in which the distinctive ideas and spirit of Jesus have broken forth again, have been the fruitful and prophetic movements in religion. Their power of attack can best be measured by the ferocity with which the Kingdom of Evil has trampled on them.

The Kingdom of God is not a concept nor an ideal merely, but an historical force. It is a vital and organizing energy now at work in humanity. Its capacity to save the social order depends on its pervasive presence within the social organism. Every institutional foothold gained gives a purchase for attacking the next vantage-point. Where a really Christian type of religious life is created, the intellect and its education are set free, and this in turn aids religion to emancipate itself from superstition and dogmatism. Where religion and intellect combine, the foundation is laid for political democracy. Where the people have the outfit and the spirit of democracy, they can curb economic exploitation. Where predatory gain and the resultant inequality are lessened, fraternal feeling and understanding become easier and the sense of solidarity grows. Where men live in the consciousness of solidarity and in the actual practice of love with their fellow-men, they are not far from the Kingdom of God. The great thing in the salvation of humanity is that salvation is present. Life begets life.

Yet it is a matter of unspeakable difficulty for the Kingdom of God to make headway against the inherent weakness of human nature and the social entrenchments of the Kingdom of Evil. "The risks of temporary disaster which great ideals run, appear to be directly proportioned to the value of the ideals. Great truths bear long sorrows." The more we do justice to this fact, the more we shall realize that the initiation and perpetuation of the historical movement of redemption was the essential thing. Jesus was the initiator. To show this more and more clearly is the service the social gospel asks of doctrinal and historical theology. By this avenue of approach we shall appreciate the human dimensions of Jesus. The individualistic theology was the creation of men with little historical training and historical consciousness, and to that extent the problems they set were the product of uneducated minds. The full greatness of the problem of Jesus strikes us when we see him in his connection with human history. Our own consciousness of God's love and forgiveness, our inward freedom, our social feeling, the set of our will toward the achievement of the Kingdom of God, our fellowship with the "two or three" in which we have a realization of the higher presence, we owe to our connection with the historical force which Jesus initiated. Where did he himself get what he had? At what fountain did he drink?

[1] Royce, " Problem of Christianity," I, 54.

but he presents Jesus as the lone ranger!

CHAPTER XV

THE SOCIAL GOSPEL AND THE CONCEPTION OF GOD

My main purpose in this book has been to show that the
social gospel is a vital part of the Christian conception of
sin and salvation, and that any teaching on the sinful
condition of the race and on its redemption from evil
which fails to do justice to the social factors and processes in sin and redemption, must be incomplete, unreal,
and misleading. Also, since the social gospel henceforth is to be an important part of our Christian message, its chief convictions must be embodied in these doctrines in some organic form.

Now, the doctrines of sin and salvation are the start-
ing-point and goal of Christian theology. Every essential change or enlargement in them is bound to affect
related doctrines also. It will be the object of the re-
maining chapters of the book to indicate how the social
gospel would re-act on the doctrine of God, of the Holy
Spirit and inspiration, of the sacraments, of eschatology,
and of the atonement.

The conception of God held by a social group is a social product. Even if it originated in the mind of a
solitary thinker or prophet, as soon as it becomes the
property of a social group, it takes on the qualities of
that group. If, for instance, a high and spiritual idea

of God is brought to a people ignorant and accustomed
to superstitious methods of winning the favour or help of
higher beings, it will soon be coarsened and materialized.
The changes in the Hebrew conception of God were the
result of the historical experiences of the nation and
its leaders. The Christian idea of God has also had its
ups and downs in the long and varied history of Christian civilization.

A fine and high conception of God is a social achievement and a social endowment. It becomes part of the
spiritual inheritance common to all individuals in that
religious group. If every individual had to work out his
idea of God on the basis of his own experiences and in-
tuitions only, it would be a groping quest, and most of us
would see only the occasional flitting of a distant light.
By the end of our life we might have arrived at the
stage of voodooism or necromancy. Entering into a high
conception of God, such as the Christian faith offers us, is
like entering a public park or a public gallery of art and
sharing the common wealth. When we learn from the
gospels, for instance, that God is on the side of the poor,
and that he proposes to view anything done or not done
to them as having been done or not done to him, such
a revelation of solidarity and humanity comes with a re-
generating shock to our selfish minds. Any one studying
life as it is on the basis of real estate and bank clearings,
would come to the conclusion that God is on the side of
the rich. It takes a revelation to see it the other way.

Wherever we encounter such a strain of social feeling
in our conceptions of God, it is almost sure to run straight

back either to Jesus or the prophets.   The Hebrew prophets were able to realize God in that way because they
were part of a nation which had preserved the traditions
of primitive fraternal democracy.   The prophets emphasized God's interest in righteousness and solidarity because they were making a fight to save their people from
the landlordism and oppression under which other peoples
have wilted and degenerated.   When, therefore, we to-
day feel the moral thrill of Hebrew theism, we are the *the*
heirs and beneficiaries of one untamed nation of moun- *poor*
tain-dwellers.   When such a conception of God is transmitted to other nations or to later times, it is the expor-
tation of the most precious commodity a nation can produce.

  On the other hand, if a conception of God originates *the*
among the exploiting classes in an age of despotism, it is *rich*
almost certain to contain germs of positive sinfulness
which will infect all to whom it is transmitted.

Christianity is an old religion.   Its youth was lived in
the midst of a matured and dying imperial despotism.   At
first it was an illegal organization, suppressed by the Empire, and in turn the Empire was described in our Apocalypse as "the Beast."   This hostility was a saving element which made the Church somewhat immune to the
despotic influences, as long as it lasted.   But in time the
Church came under the control and spiritual influence of
the upper classes, and finally of the Roman State.   We
know that the effects of this social environment were
wrought into the constitutional structure of the Church.
The Roman Catholic Church is still the religious replica
of the Roman imperial organization.   Harnack thinks

this is the characterization which comes closest to its real nature. Did this environment also influence the theological and religious conceptions about God?

Later the Western Church passed through the age of feudalism. Feudalism was a social order in which the military, judicial, and executive powers were under the control of the same class which controlled the one great source of wealth at that time, the agricultural land. What such a combination of private property power and governmental powers of coercion comes to was brought home to us by the revelations about the rubber trade in the Belgian Congo a few years ago. Of this feudal social order the Church was an integral and active part. The temper and attitude of the dominant part of the clergy was deeply affected by this social environment. Did it also shape the conception of God? Did it create habits of mind which came out in the religious appeals, the illustrations and arguments used, and the tacit presuppositions of all argument?

Our imagination has only a short reach. In conceiving a higher world we have to take the familiar properties and figures of our material world, and enlarge and refine them as best we can. As long as kings and governors were the greatest human beings in the public eye, it was inevitable that their image should be superimposed on the idea of God. Court language and obeisances were used in worship and when men reasoned about God, they took their illustrations and analogies from those who were a close second to God.

Athanasius, for instance, in order to explain how the

incarnation could save the human race from death and give immortal life, says that when a great king takes residence in one house in a city, the whole city enjoys great honour and is not in danger from any enemy or bandit invasion. In the same way the physical presence of the incarnate Logos dispelled the evil of death. This is one of the principal arguments in his mind. But in fact it is no argument at all except on monarchical assumptions.

In his epoch-making book, " Cur Deus Homo," Anselm bases his discussion on the proposition that God's " honour " has been violated by human sin. Man is wholly subject to God, and bound to fulfil all his demands. If he falls short, God is under no obligation to show him favour, and must exact satisfaction for the violation of his honour. He can not simply forgive sin. It is not enough if the sinner henceforth performs his whole duty. " Satisfaction " must be rendered by some adequate work of merit over and above the legal requirements of God. This equivalent man is unable to render. Christ is able. On this basis Anselm builds his theory of the atonement. It has often been pointed out that Anselm derived his idea of " satisfaction " from the Teutonic practice of commuting physical punishment into a financial payment.[1] I think Anselm, an Italian and a churchman, was also influenced by the " satisfactions " in the penitential practice of the Church. But beyond all these contemporary influences of law and custom was the pervasive impres-

[1] This was first established by my friend Professor Hermann Cremer in his monograph, " Die Wurzeln des anselmischen Satisfactionsbegriffes." Studien und Kritiken, 1880.

sion of autocratic power and monarchical self-assertion, which rates an offence against the members of the royal family or against the governing class far more highly than other crimes, and makes the king's " honour " a concern for which nations must go to war.

God's right of arbitrary decision, which has been asserted in many connections, runs back to the same autocratic sources. Duns Scotus and his followers even held that the death of Christ was necessary only because God declared it necessary. If he had been willing to accept the obedience of some good angel, that too would have sufficed. We are most familiar with the arbitrary power of God in the doctrine of election. The right of God to select some individuals for eternal life and leave others to eternal punishment, entirely apart from any question of personal merit or demerit, was always based on the ground of the " sovereignty " of God, that is, the divine autocracy. If a city rebelled, all lives were forfeited; if the King had only 50 councillors hung, or every tenth citizen sold into slavery, it was an act of royal clemency worthy of praise. By the fall all men were in a state of damnation; if God elected some to salvation and left the others as they were, it was divine grace; nor was he under obligation to explain his reasons in picking the favoured.

Scholastic arguments reach few people; imaginative pictures of spiritual ideas are subtle and pervasive. God was imagined far above, in an upper part of the universe, remote from humanity but looking down on us, fully aware of all we do, interfering when necessary, but very distinct. In Greek theology this distinctness was due to philosophical influences. In popular theology the remoteness of great men perhaps had more to do with shaping this idea than philosophy.

The sense of fear which has pervaded religion has doubtless been, at least in part, a psychological result of the despotic attitude of parents, of school-masters, of priests, and of officials all the way from the town beadle to the king. To uncounted people God has not been the great Comforter but the great Terror. The main concern in religion was to escape from his hands. Luther longed that he " might at last have a gracious God "— *einen gnädigen Gott;* the word is the same which was applied to princes and nobles when they were good-natured. Luther sweated with fear when he walked alongside of the body of the Lord in a Corpus Christi procession. To what extent was this due to the fact that he was constantly beaten by his parents and by his school-masters, and taught to be afraid of everything? Men enriched the Church enormously with gifts of land as insurance premiums that God would not do anything horrible to them. When farmers are afraid enough to part with land, it must be a deep fear.

The mediaeval methods of earning religious merit and of securing intercession were the product of fear and a close duplicate of the conditions existing under economic and political despotism. God was a feudal lord, holding his tenants in a grip from which there was no escape, exacting what was due to him, and putting the delinquent in a hot prison which was even worse than the terrible holes underneath the duke's castle. By special self-denial the religious peon could win " merit " to offset his delinquencies. The saints and the blessed Virgin had much merit. The Church had power to assign some of this to those who stood in with the Church. The intercession of the saints counted; every one knew that it was a great thing for a poor man if a nobleman spoke for him to the judge; it would be so in heaven too. Things go by favour; the more aristocracy, the more pull.

Thus the social relations in which men lived, affected their conceptions about God and his relations to men. Under tyrannous conditions the idea of God was necessarily tainted with the cruel hardness of society. This spiritual influence of despotism made even the face of Christ seem hard and stern. The outlook into the future life was like a glimpse into a chamber of torture. The conflict of the religion of Jesus with autocratic conceptions of God is therefore part of the struggle of humanity with autocratic economic and political conditions. This carries the social movement into theology. Theologians therewith have their share in redeeming humanity from the reign of tyranny and fear, and if we do not do our share emphatically and with a will, where do we belong, to the Kingdom of God or the Kingdom of Evil? The worst form of leaving the naked unclothed, the hungry unfed, and the prisoners uncomforted, is to leave men under a despotic conception of God and the universe; and what will the Son of Man do to us theologians when we gather at the Day of Doom? Here we see one of the highest redemptive services of Jesus to the human race. When he took God by the hand and called him " our Father," he democratized the

not for women

conception of God. He disconnected the idea from the coercive and predatory State, and transferred it to the realm of family life, the chief social embodiment of solidarity and love. He not only saved humanity; he saved God. He gave God his first chance of being loved and of escaping from the worst misunderstandings conceivable. The value of Christ's idea of the Fatherhood of God is realized only by contrast to the despotic ideas which it opposed and was meant to displace. We have classified theology as Greek and Latin, as Catholic and Protestant. It is time to classify it as despotic and democratic. From a Christian point of view that is a more decisive distinction.

Paul has preserved for us the deep impression of liberation and relief which the Christian idea of God made on him and his contemporaries: "For (when you became Christians) you did not receive the spirit of slavery to fill you with fear once more, but you received the spirit of sonship which leads us to cry, 'Our Father.'" The Gnostics, some of whom were exceedingly able minds, attracted to Christianity by its spiritual contents, believed that Christ had for the first time in cosmic history brought to mankind a revelation of the real God. All the other God-ideas had been counterfeits and caricatures imposed on humanity by lower and evil spiritual beings to enslave them. This is a striking expression of the feeling that the God mirrored in the teaching and person of Christ was in a wholly different class from all others.

Of course the Christian conception of God was not kept pure. The pall of darkness rising from despotic society constantly obscured and eclipsed it.   The imagery of coercion and tyranny always suggested itself anew. The triumph of the Christian idea of God will never be complete as long as economic and political despotism prevail.

The value of the Reformation should be re-assessed from this point of view.   Luther tore the idea of " merit " out of theology.   Christ alone had merit.   By his blood he had paid the whole debt once for all.   Man need not earn merit.   He can not earn merit.   It would be a sin for him to try.   That ended the contract labour system in religion.   God was reconciled.   He had been angry but he was now kind and ready to forgive.   The sinner need only believe and accept the great transaction made on his behalf.   That ended the reign of fear for those who understood.   The saints and their intercession were dismissed; they never had any merit either; the sinner could deal with God and Christ direct.   Purgatory was gone; only hell proper remained.   It was a religious Seisachtheia, like that in Athens under Solon's laws, a great unloading, a revolution in the field of the spiritual life, and the condition for the coming of political and economic liberty.

But the restoration of the Christian conception of God was by no means complete.   Despotic government was still in full swing when the Reformation theology was written.   Luther and Calvin were not personally in sympathy with democracy.   The age of absolutism and of Louis XIV was just ahead.   The long era of witch-trials had just begun. The spell of fear was broken only for a few. The fundamental assumptions about God remained. The inherited forensic terminology of theology suggested the old lines of thought. As long as religion borrows its terms from the procedure of law-courts, the spirit of coercion and terror leaks in. Legal ideas are not congruous with the Christian consciousness of salvation. The idea of "justification" did not come to us from Jesus and it does not blend well with his way of thinking. For Paul and Luther "justification by faith" was an emancipating idea; it stood for an immense simplification and sweetening of the process of salvation. They used the terminology of legalism to deny its spirit. To us, who are not under the consciousness of Jewish or Roman Catholic legality, "justification" does not convey the same sense of liberation, but the phrase is now a vehicle by which legal and often despotic ideas come back to plague us.

The social gospel is God's predestined agent to continue what the Reformation began. It arouses intelligent hatred of oppression and the reign of fear, and teaches us to prize liberty and to love love. Therefore those whose religious life has been influenced by the social gospel are instinctively out of sympathy with autocratic conceptions of God. They sense the spiritual taint which goes out from such ideas. They know that these religious conceptions are used to make autocratic social conditions look tolerable, necessary, and desirable. Like Paul, the social gospel has not "received the spirit of bondage again unto fear." It is wholly in sympathy with the conception of the Father which Jesus revealed to us by his words, by his personality, and by his own relations to the Father.

This reformatory and democratizing influence of the social gospel is not against religion but for it. The worst thing that could happen to God would be to remain an autocrat while the world is moving toward democracy. He would be dethroned with the rest. For one man who has forsaken religion through scientific doubt, ten have forsaken it in our time because it seemed the spiritual opponent of liberty and the working people. This feeling will deepen as democracy takes hold and becomes more than a theory of government. We have heard only the political overture of democracy, played by fifes; the economic numbers of the program are yet to come, and they will be performed with trumpets and trombones.

The Kingdom of God is the necessary background for the Christian idea of God. The social movement is one of the chief ways in which God is revealing that he lives and rules as a God that loves righteousness and hates iniquity. A theological God who has no interest in the conquest of justice and fraternity is not a Christian. It is not enough for theology to eliminate this or that autocratic trait. Its God must join the social movement. The real God has been in it long ago. The development of a Christian social order would be the highest proof of God's saving power. The failure of the social movement would impugn his existence.

The old conception that God dwells on high and is distinct from our human life was the natural basis for

autocratic and arbitrary ideas about him.   On the other
hand the religious belief that he is immanent in humanity is the natural basis for democratic ideas about him.
When he was far above, he needed vice-gerents to rule
for him, popes by divine institution and kings by divine
right.   If he lives and moves in the life of mankind, he
can act directly on the masses of men.   A God who
strives within our striving, who kindles his flame in our
intellect, sends the impact of his energy to make our will
restless for righteousness, floods our sub-conscious mind
with dreams and longings, and always urges the race on
toward a higher combination of freedom and solidarity,
— that would be a God with whom democratic and religious men could hold converse as their chief fellow-
worker, the source of their energies, the ground of their
hopes.

Platonic philosophy in the first century made God so
transcendent that it had to devise the Logos-idea to bridge
the abyss between the silent depths of God and this world,
and to enable God to create and to reveal himself.   Theology shrank from imputing suffering to God.   Patripas-
sianism seemed a self-evident heresy.   To-day men want
to think of God as close to them, and spiritually kin to
them, the Father of all spirits.   Eminent theologians insist that God has always suffered with and for mankind
and that the cross is a permanent law of God's nature:
" The lamb has been slain from the beginning of the
world."   Through the conception of evolution and
through the social movement we have come to see human
life in its totality, and our consciousness of God is the
spiritual counterpart of our social consciousness.   Some,

apparently, would be willing to think of God as less than
omnipotent and omniscient if only he were working hard
with us for that Kingdom which is the only true Democracy.

Two points still demand discussion. The first is the
problem of suffering.

The existence of innocent suffering impugns the justice
and benevolence of God, both of which are essential in a
Christian conception of God.

The simplest solution is to deny the existence of unjust
suffering; to trust that good and ill are allotted according to desert; and if the righteous Job suffers great disaster, to search for his secret sin. This explanation broke
down before the facts. How about the man born blind?
What personal sin had merited his calamity?

Dualism took the other extreme. It acknowledged
that the good suffer, and stressed the fact. But it ex-
culpated the good God by making the evil God the author
of this world, or at least its present lord.

Christianity has combined several explanations of suffering. It grounds it in general on the prevalence of sin
since the fall. It has ascribed a malignant power of
afflicting the righteous to Satan and his servants. It has
taken satisfaction when justice was vindicated in some
striking case of goodness or wickedness. It has held out
a hope of a public vindication of the righteous in the
great judgment, and of an equalization of their lot by
their bliss in heaven and the suffering of the wicked.
(This element, however, was weakened in Protestantism
by the disappearance of purgatory and the tacit assump-

tion that all who are saved at all will enjoy an equal bliss.
Purgatory was a great balancer and equalizer.) Finally,
Christianity has taught that God allots suffering with wise
and loving intent, tempering it according to our strength,
relieving it in response to our prayer, and using it to
chasten our pride, to win us from earthliness to himself,
and to prepare us for heaven. This interpretation does
not assert the justice of every suffering, taken by itself,
but does maintain its loving intention.

All these are powerful and comforting considerations.
But they are shaken by the bulk of the unjust suffering in
sight of the modern mind. These Christian ideas are
largely true as long as we look at a normal village community and its individuals and families. But they are
jarred by mass disasters. The optimism of the age of
rationalism was shaken by the Lisbon earthquake in 1755,
when 30,000 people were killed together, just and unjust.
The War has deeply affected the religious assurance of
our own time, and will lessen it still more when the ex-
citement is over and the aftermath of innocent suffering
becomes clear. But that impression of undeserved mass
misery which the war has brought home to the thought-
less, has long been weighing on all who understood the
social conditions of our civilization. The sufferings of
a single righteous man could deeply move the psalmists
or the poet of Job. To day entire social classes sit in the
ashes and challenge the justice of the God who has afflicted them by fathering the present social system. The
moral and religious problem of suffering has entered on
a new stage with the awakening of the social consciousness and the spread of social knowledge.

If God stands for the present social order, how can we defend him? We can stand the pain of travail, of physical dissolution, of earthquakes and accidents. These are the price we pay for the use of a fine planet with lovely appurtenances and for a wonderful body. We can also accept with reasonable resignation the mental anguish of unrequited love, of foiled ambition, or of the emptiness of life. These are the risks we run as possessors of a highly organized personality amid a world of men. But we can not stand for poor and laborious people being deprived of physical stature, youth, education, human equality, and justice, in order to enable others to live luxurious lives. It revolts us to see these conditions perpetuated by law and organized force, and palliated or justified by the makers of public opinion. None of the keys offered by individualistic Christianity fit this padlock.

The social gospel supplies an explanation of this class of human suffering. Society is so integral that when one man sins, other men suffer, and when one social class sins, the other classes are involved in the suffering which follows on that sin. The more powerful an individual is, the more will he involve others; the more powerful a class is, the more will it be able to unload its own just suffering on the weaker classes. These sufferings are not " vicarious "; they are solidaristic.

Our solidarity is a beneficent part of human life. It is the basis for our greatest good. If our community life is righteous and fraternal, we are enriched and enlarged by being bound up with it. But, by the same law, if our community is organized in a way that permits, encourages, or defends predatory practices, then the larger part of its members are through solidarity caged to be eaten by the rest, and to suffer what is both unjust and useless.

It follows that ethically it is of the highest importance to prevent our beneficent solidarity from being twisted into a means of torture. *— feedback systems*

Physical pain serves a beneficent purpose by warning us of the existence of abnormal conditions. It fulfils its purpose when it compels the individual to search out the cause of pain and to keep his body in health. If he takes " dope " to quiet the consciousness of pain without healing the causes, the beneficent purpose of pain is frustrated.

Social suffering serves social healing. If the sense of common humanity is strong enough to set the entire social *naive* body in motion on behalf of those who suffer without just cause, then their troubles are eased and the whole body is preserved just and fraternal. If the predatory forces are strong enough to suppress the reactions against injustice and inhumanity, the suffering goes on and the whole community is kept in suicidal evil. To interpret the sufferings imposed by social injustice in individualistic terms as the divine chastening and sanctification of all the individuals concerned, is not only false but profoundly mischievous. It is the equivalent of *good* " dope," for it silences the warning which the suffering *critique* of an innocent group ought to convey to all society without abolishing the causes. It frustrates the only chance of redemptive usefulness which the sufferers had.

All this applies to our conception of God. The idea of solidarity, when once understood, acts as a theodicy. *✕* None of us would want a world without organic com-

munity of life, any more than we would want a world
without gravitation. The fact that a careless boy falls
down stairs does not condemn gravitation, nor does the
existence of evil community life condemn God who constituted us social beings. The innocent suffering of great
groups through social solidarity simply brings home to
us that the tolerance of social injustice is an intolerable
evil. The great sin of men is to resist the reformation
of predatory society. We do not want God to be charged
with that attitude. A conception of God which describes
him as sanctioning the present social order and utilizing
it in order to sanctify its victims through their suffering,
without striving for its overthrow, is repugnant to our
moral sense. Both the Old Testament and the New Testament characterizations of God's righteousness assure
us that he hates with steadfast hatred just such practices
as modern communities tolerate and promote. If we can
trust the Bible, God is against capitalism, its methods,
spirit, and results. The bourgeois theologians have mis-
represented our revolutionary God. God is for the
Kingdom of God, and his Kingdom does not mean injustice and the perpetuation of innocent suffering. The
best theodicy for modern needs is to make this very clear.

Finally, the social gospel emphasizes the fact that God
is the bond of racial unity.

Speaking historically, it is one of the most universal
and important characteristics of religion that it constitutes the spiritual bond of social groups. A national god
was always the exponent of national solidarity. A com-

mon religion created common sympathies. Full moral obligation stopped at the religious boundary line. The unusual thing about the Good Samaritan was that he disregarded the religious cleavage and followed the call of humanity pure and simple. The mingling of populations and religions in modern life makes the influence of religion less noticeable, but it still works as a bond of sympathy. It is easiest to trace it where the religious cleavage coincides with the racial or political cleavages. The French Catholics in Quebec and the English Protestants in Ontario; the Irish and the Ulstermen; the Catholic Belgians and the Protestant Dutch; the Latin nations of America and the United States;— the mention of the names brings up the problem. The Balkans are a nest of antagonisms partly because of religious differences. It has been fortunate for the American negro that the antagonism of race and social standing has not been intensified in his case by any difference of religion.[1]

The spread of a monotheistic faith and the recognition of a single God of all mankind is a condition of an ethical union of mankind in the future. This is one of the long-range social effects of Christian missions. The effects of Christianity will go far beyond its immediate converts. Every competing religion will be compelled to emphasize its monotheistic elements and to allow its polytheistic ingredients to drop to a secondary stage.

[1] I have seen Southern pamphlets undertaking to prove that the negroes are not descended from Adam, but have evolved from African jungle beasts. The very orthodox authors were willing to accept the heretical philosophy of evolution for the black people,

But it is essential to our spiritual honesty that no imperialism shall masquerade under the cover of our religion. Those who adopt the white man's religion come under the white man's influence. Christianity is the religion of the dominant race. The native religions are a spiritual bulwark of defence, independence, and loyalty. If we invite men to come under the same spiritual roof of monotheism with us and to abandon their ancient shelters, let us make sure that this will not be exploited as a trick of subjugation by the Empires. As long as there are great colonizing imperialisms in the world, the propaganda of Christianity has a political significance.

God is the common basis of all our life. Our human personalities may seem distinct, but their roots run down into the eternal life of God. In a large way both philosophy and science are tending toward a recognition of the truth which religion has felt and practised. The all-pervading life of God is the ground of the spiritual oneness of the race and of our hope for its closer fellowship in the future.

The consciousness of solidarity, therefore, is of the essence of religion. But the circumference and spaciousness of the fellowship within it differ widely. Every discovery of a larger fellowship by the individual brings a glow of religious satisfaction. The origin of the Christian religion was bound up with a great transition from a nationalistic to an international religious consciousness. Paul was the hero of that conquest. The Christian God

though of course they claimed biblical creation for the white. The purpose of this religious manœuvre is to cut the bond of human obligation and solidarity established by religion, and put the negroes outside the protection of the moral law.

has been a breaker of barriers from the first. All who have a distinctively Christian experience of God are committed to the expansion of human fellowship and to the overthrow of barriers. To emphasize this and bring it home to the Christian consciousness is part of the mission of the social gospel, and it looks to theology for the intellectual formulation of what it needs.

We have discussed three points in this chapter: how the conception of God can be cleansed from the historic accretions of despotism and be democratized; how it can be saved from the indictment contained in the unjust suffering of great social groups; and how we can realize God as the ground of social unity. Freedom, justice, solidarity are among the aims of the social gospel. It needs a theology which will clearly express these in its conception of God.

CHAPTER XVI

THE HOLY SPIRIT, REVELATION, INSPIRATION, PROPHECY

THE doctrine of the Holy Spirit is one of the most religious of all Christian doctrines. It is not primarily a product of reflection, but of the great religious emotions and experiences. Perhaps for that very reason it has been relatively a neglected section of doctrinal theology. It deals with the most intimate and mystic experiences of the soul, and does not seem to belong to the field especially cultivated by the social gospel.

But in fact the social nature of religion is clearly demonstrated in the work of the Holy Spirit. The prophets of the Old Testament were not lonely torches set aflame by the spirit of God; they were more like a string of electric lights along a road-side, which, though far apart, are all connected and caused by the same current. They transmitted not only their ideas but their spiritual receptivity and inspiration to one another. The great men of whom we think as solitary miracles of religious power were surrounded and upborne in their day by religious groups which have now melted back into oblivion. Their prophetic consciousness was awakened and challenged by historic events affecting the social group to which they belonged. "The burden of the Lord" was not for themselves but for their community. They knew that their revelation was to be a message.   Their religious experiences were moments of intense social consciousness.

The Christian Church began its history as a community of inspiration.   The new thing in the story of Pentecost is not only the number of those who received the tongue of fire but the fact that the Holy Spirit had become the common property of a group.   What had seemed to some extent the privilege of aristocratic souls was now democratized.   The spirit was poured on all flesh; the young saw visions, the old dreamed dreams; even on the slave class the spirit was poured.   The charismatic life of the primitive Church was highly important for its coherence and loyalty in the crucial days of its beginning.   It was a chief feeder of its strong affections, its power of testimony, and its sacrificial spirit.   Religion has been defined as " the life of God in the soul of man."   In Christianity it became also the life of God in the fellowship of man.   The mystic experience was socialized.

The doctrine of the inspiration of the Bible, as we all know, has passed through profound changes in recent years.   The change has all been away from religious individualism and toward a social comprehension of the religious facts.

The process of inspiration was formerly conceived as a transaction between God and the individual.   The higher the doctrine of inspiration, the more solitary was the inspired individual.   It would have defeated the purpose of the doctrine to admit the presence of outside influences. Even the intellect and personality of the recipient were sometimes represented as passive and quiescent. Philo, whose ideas the early Church followed, said: "A prophet gives forth nothing at all of his own, but acts as interpreter at the prompting of another in all his utterances, and as long as he is under inspiration he is in ignorance, his reason departing from its place, and yielding up the citadel of the soul, when the divine Spirit enters into it and strikes at the mechanism of the voice." In extreme orthodoxy it was a liberal concession to grant that the divine power utilized and respected the literary style and individual outlook of the writer.

The modern conception of inspiration not only recognizes the free operation and the contributions of the distinctive psychical equipment of the inspired person, but seeks in every way to get beyond the individual to the social group which produced him, to the spiritual predecessors who inspired him, and to the audience which moved him because he hoped to move it. We might characterize the progress of the historical study of religion in the last fifty years as a progressive effort to interpret religious individuals by their social contacts. The great work of biblical criticism has been to place every biblical book in its exact historical environment as a preliminary to understanding its religious message. The "*religionsgeschichtliche Methode*" takes up the work where the critical method drops it, and reaches out still further, beyond the ideas and purposes of the literary person to the religious drifts and desires and beliefs of his age, to which he more or less consciously reacted.

Every one who has shared in the results of this work will appreciate how helpful and fruitful this process at its best has been. It has opened up the inspiration of the past and released social values which had been completely locked away under the individualistic method of interpretation. The historical method has already done what the social gospel might wish it to do. Here we have a completed laboratory experiment proving the value and efficiency of a social understanding of religion. The only question is whether we can win just as strong a sense of the presence of God from this complicated social process of inspiration, as when God was believed to have dictated the books by a psychological miracle. It can be done, but the interpreter needs personal acquaintance with inspiration to do it.

In another direction, however, we have not yet overcome the narrowing influence of the old, mechanical views of inspiration.

Those who have had first-hand experience of inspiration either in their own souls or in the life of others, have always combined reverence for the authority of the word of the Lord and a realization of the human frailty and liability to error in the prophet. Paul and his churches had a rich experience of inspiration. Writing to the Thessalonians he asserts the right of prophesying, but takes the duty of critical scrutiny by the hearers as a matter of course: "Quench not the spirit (in yourselves); despise not prophesying (in others); scrutinize all utterances; appropriate what is good." Inspiration did not involve infallibility when men knew it by experience.

When the inspirationalism of the primitive Church died

out, the understanding of its nature grew artificial, just as the understanding of Old Testament inspiration had become centuries earlier.   It was not to the interest of church leaders to emphasize that the laity had once possessed the gift of inspiration and the right of utterance. Consequently the realization of the charismatic life of the primitive Church was allowed to fade from the memory of Christians.   The apostles alone stood out in the historical perspective as the possessors of inspiration. Their human frailties and fallibilities were forgotten or suppressed; they were conventionalized and fitted with haloes.   Their utterances were infallible.   Inspiration and infallibility were almost convertible terms.   Being so high a gift, inspiration was strictly circumscribed, and was supposed to have ceased when the canon of the New Testament was completed.   This, on the whole, has remained the popular orthodox view down to recent times.

Now, so high a conception of inspiration discourages the stirring of the prophetic spirit in living men.   A man might well claim that God had spoken to his soul and laid a message upon him.   But who would want to claim that he is infallible?   Psychical experiences are evoked by expectancy.   If men do not expect to be regenerated, few will have the experience.   If they do not expect to be inspired, few will make their way single-handed to such an experience.   The Church has reversed all the maxims of Paul except the last.   It has quenched the spirit; it has discountenanced prophesying; it has forbidden intellectual scrutiny of inspiration so far as the biblical books were concerned.   The only thing it encouraged was to cleave to that which is good.

The old view of inspiration is supposed to be more deeply religious than the new. It did involve a more reverent and passive attitude of mind. But it robbed us of part of our consciousness of God. A religious man knows that he has no merit of his own, and that all his righteousness was wrought in him by God. To suppose that he can set his own will on God and work out his own salvation is sub-christian. We ought to have the same consciousness of God's influence on our intellectual comprehension of Christian truth. To suppose that we can work out a living knowledge of the truth from a sacred book without the enlightening energy of the spirit of God is sub-christian and rationalistic. On the other hand, to be conscious of the divine light, to listen to the inner voice, to read the inspired words of the Bible with an answering glow of fire, is part of the consciousness of God to which we are entitled. There are many degrees of clarity and power in this living inspiration, and heavy admixtures of human error, passion, and false sentiment, but the same is true of the experiences of regeneration and sanctification. It is the business of the Church to encourage, temper, and purify the intellectual, as well as the emotional and volitional experiences of its members.

At this point the social gospel coincides with the most energetic religious consciousness. Traditional theology has felt the need of inspired prophets and apostles chiefly in order to furnish the system of doctrine with a firm footing of inerrancy and infallibility. The doctrine of inspiration is not treated as part of the glorious results of redemption, and as the Christian salvation of the human intellect, but as part of the prolegomena of theology. The social gospel, on the other hand, feels the need of present inspiration and of living prophetic spirits in order to lead humanity toward the Kingdom of God. Wherever the Church is set in the centre and her aim is to keep the body of doctrine intact as delivered to it, inspiration will be located at the beginning of the line of tradition, and at most the power of infallible interpretation will be claimed for popes and church councils. Wherever the Kingdom of God is set to the front, inspiration will spontaneously spring into life at the points where the conflict is hot and active in the present. A theology adapted to the social gospel, therefore, will recognize inspiration as an indispensable force of our religion and an essential equipment of redemption. The social order can not be saved without regenerate men; neither can it be saved without inspired men.

The value of the regenerate individual for the advancement of the Kingdom of God consists largely in his prophetic quality. If the Holy Spirit works on his soul so that he has a vision of the Kingdom of God and its higher laws, then to some extent he will be living ahead of his age. In the qualities of his personality and in his judgments of men and events he will.be a witness to the divine order of society, and will challenge the right of the world as it now is. If this prophetic insight is not dulled by ignorance and made erratic by eccentricities of character, but is guided by education and balance of character, its social force is very great.

Individualistic religion has bred saints, missionaries, pastors, and scholars, but few prophets. Some of its so-called prophets have been expounders of the prophecy of others. Religions of authority have no real use for prophets except to furnish a supernatural basis for doctrine. Hence prophecy used to be put on a level with miracles as "evidences of the Christian religion." Where the main interest is to keep doctrine undisturbed, living prophecy seems a dangerous and unsettling force.

Genuine prophecy springs up where fervent religious experience combines with a democratic spirit, strong social feeling, and free utterance. Some sense of antagonism between the will of God and the present order of things is necessary to ignite the spirit of the prophet.

This was the combination which produced the Hebrew prophets. We have the same combination in those manifold radical bodies which preceded and accompanied the Reformation. They all tended toward the same type, the type of primitive Christianity. Strong fraternal feeling, simplicity and democracy of organization, more or less communistic ideas about property, an attitude of passive obedience or conscientious objection toward the coercive and militaristic governments of the time, opposition to the selfish and oppressive Church, a genuine faith in the practicability of the ethics of Jesus, and, as the secret power in it all, belief in an inner experience of regeneration and an inner light which interprets the outer word of God. These radical bodies did not produce as many great individuals as we might have expected because their intellectuals and leaders were always killed off or silenced. But their communities were prophetic. They have been the forerunners of the modern world. They stood against war, against capital punishment, against slavery, and against coercion in matters of religion before others thought of it. It was largely due to their influence that the Puritan Revolution had its prophetic elements of leadership. The Free Churches throughout the world, consciously or unconsciously, clearly or dimly, have passed beyond the official types of orthodox Protestantism and have taken on some of the characteristics of the early radicals. Great church bodies now stand as a matter of course on those principles of freedom and toleration which only the boldest once dared to assert. The power of leadership is with those organizations and movements which have some prophetic qualities and trust to the inner light.

To-day it is the social gospel which has the democratic outlook and the sense of solidarity. If it also has spiritual fervor, it will have prophetic power.

The social gospel is not a doctrine turned backward to the sources of authority, but a faith turned forward to its task. It sees before it the Kingdom of Evil to be overcome, and the Kingdom of God to be established, and it cries aloud for an inspired word of God to give faith and power and guidance. If theology is to answer to the needs of the social gospel, it ought to assign to prophecy a definite place among the permanent forces of redemption. In recognizing the need of inspiration and prophecy the social gospel is more religious than the orthodox type, and more positive than that liberal type of theology which is chiefly interested in historical criticism.[1]

[1] I shall return to this subject once more at the end of the last chapter.

CHAPTER XVII

THE sacraments have occupied a large place in the worship and life of the Church, and a correspondingly wide room in theology. The Catholic Church is the institution of sacramental salvation. The Reformation was in large part a movement for cleansing the sacramental practices and doctrines. The disastrous split between the Lutheran and Zwinglian churches was due to differences about the significance of one of the sacraments. Large historical denominational bodies have formed about the effort to restore the genuine practice and doctrine of baptism. Evidently the conception of the sacraments has long been an active volcanic region in theology. The old controversial zeal has been followed by relative apathy. Except under " High Church " influences the importance of the sacraments in practical church life seems to be lessening and the issues are being forgotten.

Can the religious spirit of the social gospel give any fresh spiritual meaning to the ancient ordinances, or add anything to the theological interpretation of them? I confess I doubt it. The two fields of interest lie far apart at present. But as a challenge to thought perhaps the following considerations may have some use.

When the act of baptism was initiated by John the Baptist and continued for a time by Jesus, it was not a ritual act of individual salvation, but an act of dedication to a religious and social movement. Baptism at the Jordan was not received to save the individual by himself, or in a future life; it was received in view of the impending Messianic salvation and as an act of allegiance to a new order of things. The baptism of John can not be separated from his preaching; the former received its meaning and content from the latter. His preaching called men to repent of their old way of living, to quit grafting, and to begin to live in fraternal helpfulness. Baptism was the dramatic expression of an inward consent and allegiance to the higher standards of life which were to prevail in the Messianic community. It was the symbol of a revolutionary movement.

There is no indication that Jesus or his disciples practised baptism during the Galilean period of his work. When the practice was resumed by the primitive Church, it was once more an act of obedience and faith in view of the impending Messianic Kingdom at the return of the Lord. The ritual act now got its ethical interpretation from the remembered sayings of the Master and from the fraternal life of the Christian group.

Baptism was profoundly affected by the great change which came over Christianity when it left its Jewish environment and was assimilated by Greek religious and social life. It was gradually filled with new meanings. It was an act cancelling the guilt of all past sins; an act of regeneration; an act of exorcization, cleansing from the defilement of pagan worship and life. But it was less and less a dedication to the coming Kingdom of God. It still had a great social significance, for it was the act by which the individual stepped out of pagan society and into the fellowship of the Christian group, with its love, its dangers, and its limitations.

This change in the meaning and content of baptism was confirmed by the spread of infant baptism since the middle of the second century. The immediate cause for the baptism of young children was the belief that baptism is necessary for salvation, combined with the ever urgent facts of infant mortality. Origen, and still more Augustine, tied up the church practice with the doctrine of original sin. Baptism had been the symbol of a revolutionary hope, an ethical act which determined the will and life of the person receiving it. It was now a ceremony performed on a babe to save it from the guilt and power of original sin and to assure its salvation in heaven in case of its death.

Here again new social elements sprang up. The practical necessities of the case created a social backing for the young candidate. Since his own responses were still inarticulate, grown-up sponsors recited the creed and other formulas for him, and this service established a social relationship which often lasted for life. Since the faith of the child was still undeveloped, theology taught that the sponsors and the Church were to supply it.

In modern time much finer ideas have been attached to infant baptism. The act is based on the organic unity of the family; the parents thereby dedicate the child to God and pledge themselves to give it Christian nurture; the child is by baptism incorporated into the organism of the Church and made to share in its saving power; the act ex-

presses the consciousness of the Church that the child is
a child of God and has a right to claim the divine pater-
nity.   These are much more Christian ideas than those
which first called infant baptism into existence.

Scarcely any Christian institution has experienced such
changes and deteriorations as baptism, but of them all
the loss of outlook toward the Kingdom of God was one
of the most regrettable.   Could the social gospel — at
least in some instances — fill baptism with its original
meaning?   We could imagine a minister and a group of
candidates who unite in feeling the evil of the present
world-order and the promise and claims of the impending Christian world-order, together using baptism to express their solemn dedication to the tasks of the Kingdom
of God, and accepting their rights as children of God
within that Kingdom.   In those churches in which baptism is administered in infancy, confirmation would offer the next best opportunity to impress and express such
convictions.   In the catechumenate the ancient Church
put the candidate through long processes of exorcization
to expel the demon powers which had infected him in his
pagan life.   Those churches which practise confirmation
have shifted the instruction of the catechumenate to pre-
cede confirmation; those churches which practise adult
baptism are much in need of a period of systematic
instruction before baptism.   It would be a really rational
and Christian form of exorcization to break the infection
of the sinful and illusive world-order and to explain the
nature of a distinctively Christian order of life.
Such a restoration of its earliest meaning might save

baptism from the religious and theological emptiness
which now threatens its very existence. Its older doctrinal meanings have leaked away or evaporated. In the
ancient Church it was closely connected with the prevalent belief in demonism. Patristic and scholastic
theology bound it up with original sin. But we do not
live in a realizing sense of demon powers, and original
sin and baptismal regeneration seem to be marked for
extinction. To say that Christ commanded it and that
we must obey his ordinance, is equivalent to confessing
that the act has lost its enthusiasm and its religious conviction. It is simply an order, which must be obeyed.
Why not connect baptism with the Kingdom of God?
It has always been an exit and an entrance; why not the
exit from the Kingdom of Evil and the entrance into the
Kingdom of God? That would, under right teaching
and with the right people, give it solemn impressiveness.
It would make it a truly Christian act. Baptism has always been dogged by superstitions, and thrust down into
paganism. The individualistic interpretation of it as an
escape from damnation tainted it with selfishness. Contact with the Kingdom of God would restore baptism
to its original ethical and spiritual purity.

The Lord's Supper, like Baptism, has had a tragic
history.

The meal in the upper room at Jerusalem was the last
of many meals in which Jesus had broken the bread
with his friends in the close intimacy of their wandering
life. The spirit of all the previous meals was in this
last meal. It was pervaded by the same strong and

holy feelings of friendship which make the disappointment of Jesus in the garden so pathetic. It is a question whether Jesus' thought ran beyond the group of his friends when he asked for a repetition of the meal; it seems at least very unlikely that he purposed a cult act such as actually developed. His purpose was to create an act of loyalty which would serve to keep memory and fidelity alive until he should return and eat and drink with them again in the Kingdom of God. Jesus had created a wonderful social group. He wanted it to hold together. The Lord's Supper came into existence through strong religious and social feeling and its purpose was the maintenance of the highest loyalty.

In the primitive Church the memorial act was part of a fraternal meal in which the Christian group met in religious privacy to express its peculiar unity and coherence. Such communistic meals, to which every member contributed his portion of food, were quite common among the religious and fraternal societies of the time. Communistic meals produce solidaristic feelings even today. Paul was not a marked exponent of democratic emotions, but he was deeply shocked when he learned that the social character of the common meal at Corinth had been debased by the intrusion of the class divisions of the outside world. The welltodo gathered in coteries to eat their plentiful supplies, while the poor sat neglected and ashamed. His feeling testifies to the social beauty and power which the Lord's Supper then possessed. (I Cor. xi, 17–34.)

There can be no doubt that the Lord's Supper has always had a powerful influence in consolidating the fraternal organization of the Church. It has always been an inner privilege, for which preparation had to be made, and from which a man might be excluded; consequently it was prized. In the European State Churches, people who have become wholly indifferent to church life, still attend communion once a year and would regard it as a loss to be shut out from it. In the early Church, discipline consisted largely in barring offenders from communion. The humiliation and sacrifices assumed by penitents in order to get back into the full solidarity of the Church shows that strong social feelings were at work here. Reconciliation among the members preceded communion. None could share in the Lord's Supper who were in a state of enmity with other Christians. Thus people were compelled to face Christ's law of love and forgiveness, and pluck the bitter root of pride and ill-will from their hearts. This, too, was a social value of the ceremony. The rubric of the Book of Common Prayer still empowers the minister to warn notorious offenders to stay away, and to do the same "with those, betwixt whom he perceiveth malice and hatred to reign, not suffering them to be partakers of the Lord's Table, until he know them to be reconciled." This is expressed also in the beautiful invitation:

"Ye who do truly and earnestly repent you of your sins, and are in love and charity with your neighbours, and intend to lead a new life, following the commandments of God, and walking from henceforth in his holy ways: Draw near with faith, and take this holy sacrament to your comfort, and make your humble confession to Almighty God, devoutly kneeling."

In the first generation, and perhaps later, the Lord's Supper still had an outlook toward the coming of the Lord. We find this still in a significant phrase in Paul, who otherwise emphasized other lines of thought: " For as often as ye eat this bread and drink this cup, ye proclaim the Lord's death *till he come."* Now, to the larger part of the primitive Church the coming of the Lord signified the coming of the millennial reign of peace and righteousness on earth. The Lord's Supper was, therefore, connected with the realization of the social ideals and hopes of the Church. The prevalence of prophecy in the charismatic life of primitive Christianity points in the same direction. It acted as an interpretation of the Lord's Supper.

The outlook toward the coming of the Lord became dim as time went on. The eucharistic act was cut loose from the fraternal meal, and that was a great lessening of its social value. The meal was still held occasionally in the evening, but turned into a charitable performance where the rich fed the poor, and it finally ceased. The eucharistic act was connected with the church worship on Sunday morning. It developed sacramental qualities in two directions; it was mystic food, in which the Lord was present and through which his grace and power and immortal life nourished the soul; and it was a sacrifice offered to God. The fact that it was the central mystery of the esoteric ritual of the church made it very important as a bond of unity, but the fraternal feeling of the early days was lessened. It intensified the consciousness of God rather than the consciousness of man. The fraternal meal of Jesus became a chief means of creating the priesthood of the Catholic Church, and the main door through which superstitious beliefs came in. In time it became the mass, in which the priest partook of the bread and wine while the people watched him doing it. He might even go through the whole performance alone, for the benefit of a deceased person, according to the terms of an endowment. Thus the Lord's Supper lost its meaning because it was in the hands of a body which had neither social outlook nor democratic emotions.

The Protestant Reformation concentrated on the re-form of the Lord's Supper. The laity shared more fully in it. The private mass was abolished. Some of the social feeling was restored. But not the social out-look. The act turned backward and not forward. It is an act of remembrance; in it we appropriate the aton-ing death of our Saviour. Where it is experienced most deeply, it is a mystic act of fellowship between the un-seen Lord and the silent soul of the worshipper.

For a time the great act of fraternal love became the object of bitter controversial feelings between Catholic and Protestant, and between Lutheran and Calvinist, and exercised a very unsocial and divisive influence.

While the great churches were bitterly contending over the question whether their Lord was physically or spiritually present, and if physically, whether by tran-substantiation or consubstantiation, the persecuted Ana-baptists, who had neither the right to meet nor to exist, had the spirit of the original institution among them. As in the primitive Church, their service was preceded by searching of heart and reconciliation, so that all might be one in Christ. As in the upper room at Jerusalem, they acted in full view of death, and their main thought was to gain strength for imprisonment and torture by once more touching the garment-hem of their Lord. They often dwelt on the fact that many grains of wheat had been crushed and had felt the heat of the oven to make this bread, and many berries of the vine had been pressed in the wine-press to make this wine; in the same way the followers of Jesus must pass through affliction and persecution in order to form the body of the Lord. Thus these poor proletarians, hunted by the tyrannical combinations of Church and State, Catholic and Protestant alike, returned to the original spirit of the Lord's Meal and realized that Real Presence about which others wrangled.

Can the social gospel contribute to make the Lord's Supper more fully an act of fraternity and to connect it again with the social hope of the Kingdom of God?

In the Lord's Supper we re-affirm our supreme allegiance to our Lord who taught us to know God as our common father and to realize that all men are our brethren. In the midst of a world full of divisive selfishness we thereby accept brotherhood as the ruling principle of our life and undertake to put it into practice in our private and public activities. We abjure the selfish use of power and wealth for the exploitation of our fellows. We dedicate our lives to establishing the Kingdom of God and to winning mankind to its laws. In contemplation of the death of our Lord we accept the possibility of risk and loss as our share of service. We link ourselves to his death and accept the obligation of the cross.

It is open to any minister to emphasize thoughts such as these, connecting the Lord's Supper with the Kingdom of God. All who have the new social consciousness would feel their appeal. Any person encountering antagonism or loss for the sake of the Kingdom would find comfort and strength in connecting his troubles with the cross of Christ. The Lord's Supper was instituted by Jesus in full view of his death. We can fully share his spirit only when we too confront the possibility of suffering in the same cause.

The emphasis on such thoughts would be the reaction of the social gospel on the religious and theological content of the Lord's Supper. They would be a challenge to the Church to realize its mission as the social embodiment of the Christ-spirit in humanity. They would constitute a spiritual preparation for the actual experience of the Real Presence — that Presence which requires a social group of two or three because love and the sense of solidarity are necessary to enable him to be in the midst of us.

CHAPTER XVIII

ESCHATOLOGY

ESCHATOLOGY raises two questions of profound interest to the human mind. First, What is the future of the individual after his brief span of years on earth is over? Second, What is to be the ultimate destiny of the human race? *the planet earth?*

These questions are important to every thoughtful mind, and they are inseparable from religion. Religion is always eschatological. Its characteristic is faith. It lives in and for the future. In all other parts of our life we deal with imperfect things, fluctuating, conditioned, relative, and never complete. In religion we seek for the final realities, the absolute values, the things as God sees them, complete, in organic union.

All religions of higher development have some mythology about the future. The Christian religion needs a Christian eschatology. To be satisfying to the Christian consciousness any teaching concerning the future life of the individual must express that high valuation of the eternal worth of the soul which we have learned from Christ, and must not contradict or sully the revelation of the justice, love, and forgiving mercy of our heavenly Father contained in his words, his life, and his personality. Any doctrine about the future of the race which is to guide our thought and action, must view it from distinctively Christian, ethical points of view, and must not contradict what is historically and scientifically certain.

In fact, however, our traditional eschatology never was a purely Christian product, growing organically from Christian soil and expressing distinctively Christian convictions. It is more in the nature of an historical mosaic combining fragments of non-christian and pre-christian systems with genuine Christian ideas. It took shape under special historical conditions, and was broken up and shaped afresh to express other conditions, but in no case was it shaped to suit our modern needs. Like all eschatologies it expresses ideas about the universe, but these cosmic conceptions are pre-scientific. The world protrayed in them is the world of the Ptolemaic system, a world three stories high, with heaven above and hell beneath. During the formative centuries the Oriental and Greek religious life, which deeply influenced Christianity, was dualistic, and whatever influences have come from that source are not only historically but essentially unchristian. A Christian mind can get most satisfaction by contemplating how the genius of the Christian religion took this heterogeneous and often alien material and made something approximately Christian of it after all.

As a consequence eschatology is usually loved in inverse proportion to the square of the mental diameter of those who do the loving. Calvin was the greatest exegete of his day and he wrote commentaries on nearly all the books of the Old and New Testaments, but he gave the Apocalypse a wide berth. No interpretation of this main biblical source ever won general consent as long as it was interpreted doctrinally. The wise threw up their hands; those who devoted their minds to it, often suffered from mild obsession. Our generation is the first in eighteen hundred years to understand this book as its author, or authors, meant it to be understood, and now it is one of the most enlightening and interesting books of them all. In primitive Christianity eschatology was in the centre of religious interest and thought. Today it is on the circumference, and with some Christians it lies outside the circumference. Theologians of liberal views are brief or apologetic when they reach eschatology. This situation is deeply regrettable. Perhaps no other section of theology is so much in need of a thorough rejuvenation.

Those who believe in the social gospel are especially concerned in this element of weakness in theology. The social gospel seeks to develop the vision of the Church toward the future and to co-operate with the will of God which is shaping the destinies of humanity. It would be aided and reinforced by a modern and truly Christian conception about the future of mankind. At present no other theological influence so hampers and obstructs the social gospel as that of eschatology. All considerations taken from the life of the twentieth century cry out for something like the social gospel; but the ideas of the first century contained in eschatology are used to veto it. Those who have trained their religious thinking on the Hebrew prophets and the genuine teachings of Jesus are for the social gospel; those who have trained it on apocalyptic ideas are against it. This is all the more pathetic because the pre-millennial scheme is really an outline of the social salvation of the race. Those who hold it exhibit real interest in social and political events. But they are best pleased when they see humanity defeated and collapsing, for then salvation is nigh. Active work for the salvation of the social order before the coming of Christ is not only vain but against the will of God. Thus eschatology defeats the Christian imperative of righteousness and salvation.

Historical science and the social gospel together may be able to affect eschatology for good. Historical criticism by itself makes it look imbecile and has no creative power. The social gospel has that moral earnestness and religious faith which exerts constructive influence on doctrine.

In the first place, the social gospel can at least give us a sympathetic understanding and right valuation of some of the elements contained in the inherited body of ideas. A merely theological comprehension of it is a false understanding. It must be understood historically in connection with the social situations which created its parts, like the buildings on an old college campus, or like the Constitution and its amendments.

Those parts of Christian eschatology which deal with the future of the race are on the whole derived from Judaism, and we owe their ethical qualities to the valiant democratic spirit of the prophets. Their "Day of Yahveh" became our "Great Judgment"; the time of peace and righteousness which was to follow it became the Christian millennium. The whole was originally the religious equivalent of a wholesome revolution in which the oppressing class is eliminated and the righteous poor get relief. This central section of Christian eschatology was the product of the brave fight which Jehovah and his people made together for the ancestral freedom of the common people. The idea of a resurrection of the dead did not come into eschatology through growing individualism, but out of the feeling that the righteous who had died before the inauguration of the new order were entitled to a share in the common happiness. Demonology and satanology, which pervaded Jewish eschatology after the exile, were, as we have pointed out, in part a religious expression of social and political hatred and despair.

Those parts of eschatology which deal with the future of the individual were in the main derived from contemporary Greek life. Greek religion was characterized by a profound desire for immortality and an equally deep sense of the sin and sadness of this earthly life. The " mysteries " ministered to this desire; Christianity did it more effectively. In turn these religious desires brought out and strengthened those eschatological facts and ideas in Christianity which could serve them. Here we have one chief cause for the increasing other-worldliness of Christianity. Now, this attitude of weariness and resignation, which led to the immense popularity of ascetic ideals of life, was in part a product of the Roman Empire. It had clamped down its bureaucracy and its tax-gathering apparatus on all Mediterranean civilization; the method was political subjugation; the aim was economic exploitation. The self-government of the

Greek states by which the citizens might have been protected, had been put under safe control. Revolt was useless. If we imagine a single empire today permanently holding the seas and continents in its grip, and enriching its aristocracy from the industry of others, with every way of escape barred, we shall understand the apathy of men under the Roman Empire. The escape into immortality was the only way to freedom left to all. This social condition left deep traces in Christian eschatology.

Thus social causes contributed to the origin of eschatological ideas. Other social causes led to their disappearance. Amid the doctrinal changes of the Protestant Reformation eschatology remained unchanged except that purgatory was cut out. It had no support in the canonical Scriptures. That was one motive. But, also, the belief in purgatory had become a prolific source of income for the Church. Hell was unalterable; no gifts or indulgences could unlock its gates. The penalties to be absolved in purgatory could be lightened by indulgence, and shortened by the prayers and pious works of friends. The indulgence system was built on this belief, and innumerable endowments were provided for masses to be read for the repose of the souls in purgatory. Now, the income bearing property of the Church and the clergy living on it constituted the greatest social and economic problem of the age before the Reformation. Wherever the Reformation received the support of government, church property was " secularized " or confiscated. When Protestant theology denied the existence of purgatory, it denied that the Church could render any quid pro quo for its vested incomes, and this weakened the legal and moral hold of the Church on its endowments, and cut under some of the most offensive practices of the Church. Unless these practical considerations had made purgatory a social issue, it may be questioned whether the lack of biblical support for the doctrine would have sufficed to suppress it. The resulting contest of Protestant theology against the doctrine of purgatory induced it, by its necessary reactions, to assert that the fate of the soul is fixed at death and the saved enter into glory.

Perhaps the modern hesitancy about the doctrine of hell also has social causes. Despotic governments formerly accustomed men to frequent, public, and very horrible executions, and to long and hopeless imprisonments. Since the spread of democracy has somewhat weakened the cruel grip of the governing classes, the criminal law has become more humane. Capital punishments have become less frequent, less public, and less cruel. The outfit of prisons has improved. There is an increasing feeling that punishment should not be merely vindictive and terrifying, but remedial and disciplinary, aiming at the salvation and social restoration of the offender. Our prisons are our human hells, where men are cut off from all that exercises a saving influence on our lives — the love of wife and child and home, work and play, contact with nature, hope, ambition,— only fear and coercion are in full force. If democracy should further weaken the hold of the governing classes on the penal system of the country; and if Christianity should im-

press us with the divine worth of " the least of these "
in prison and our obligation to offer them salvation; and
if the prison system becomes redemptive; can theology
then continue to get the moral approval of mankind for a
divine prison which is not educational and redemptive,
but wholly without change or end?

Thus eschatology has all along been influenced by social
causes, while keeping on its own conservative path of
tradition. The Jewish people under social and political
oppression, and the primitive Church under persecution
wept and prayed our eschatology into existence. Our
Apocalypse is wet with human tears and must be read
that way. Ever since, some sections of eschatology
have been vivified, others modified, and some consigned
to oblivion through the pressure of social causes. Has
not the social consciousness of our age, speaking through
the social gospel, also a right to be heard in the shaping
of eschatology?

Any reformatory force taking hold of eschatology can
not expect a fresh start, but must reckon with its traditional contents and its biblical and theological sources.
It may clear our path to lay down several propositions
about this material coming from the past.

1. In everything contributed by the Old Testament we
should seek to distinguish what is due to the divine in
spiration of the prophets. We are under no obligation
to accept the mythical ideas and cosmic speculations of
the Hebrew people, their limited geography, their primitive astronomy, the historical outlook of the book of
Daniel, or the Babylonian and Persian ideas which

flowed into their religious thought. What has authority for us is the ethical and religious light of men who had an immediate consciousness of the living God, and saw him now and hereafter acting for righteousness, for the vindication of the oppressed classes, and for the purging of the social life of the nation. These elements of the Old Testament carry authority because they are in spiritual consensus with the revelation of God in Christ.

2. We should learn to distinguish clearly between prophecy and apocalypticism. There is as much difference between them as between Paul and Pope Gregory I. From apocalypticism we get the little diagrams which map out the history of the human race on deterministic methods, as if God consulted the clock. From the same source the active belief in demonology, the reliance on miraculous catastrophes, and the blue light of unreality have always come into eschatology. Those who fill their minds with it, thereby tie themselves to all backward things. Apocalyptic believers necessarily insist on the verbal inerrancy of Scripture and oppose historical methods, for their work consists in piecing mosaics of texts. Historically we can appreciate the religious value of apocalypticism in later Judaism, just as we can appreciate the religious value of the belief in transubstantiation or of scholastic theology. But as a present-day influence in religion it is dangerous. It has probably done more to discredit eschatology than any other single influence.

3. In the New Testament it is our business to sift out what is distinctively Christian in origin and spirit. It stands to reason that the leaven of the Christian spirit

was not able at once to transform the inherited ideas of Jews and Gentiles of the first generation. For instance, Christianity had to struggle hard with the stubborn nationalistic pride of Judaism which claimed either a monopoly of messianic salvation or at least special privileges within it. Even Paul, the chief exponent of international religion, could not get away from his pro-Jewish feelings, and thought God was saving the Gentiles in order to stir up the Jews and get them saved. Jesus did not make the judgment depend on nationality but on the sense of human solidarity, and repeatedly foreshadowed that the Jews would be supplanted. In the Apocalypse we are carried back into Jewish feeling and points of view. The mind of Jesus Christ is our criterion for an ethical scrutiny of these ingredients.

4. The effort to systematize the eschatological statements of biblical writers has always been muddled by the supposition that they all thought alike. There was, as yet, no orthodoxy. All were deeply interested in these questions, and men of strong conviction made their own formulations. The Apocalypse, Paul, and the fourth gospel are strikingly unlike.

The Apocalypse expounds the old social hope of Israel. The great woes and the overthrow of the mystic Babylon have political significance. There are a thousand years of messianic peace on this earth. Even after the last eruption of Satan and the great judgment the new earth is still on the old earth; the new Jerusalem comes down here, and there are trees, and a river, and happy people.

Paul, on the other hand, has no room for a millennium of flesh and blood men on a material earth.   The coming of Christ would usher in a cosmic change; the material world would end and the groaning of dying creation would cease; the living and the dead would receive spiritual bodies; therewith the last enemy, Death, would be overcome, and God would be all in all.   In Paul the Jewish and the Greek streams of thought join.   Probably in this, as in other things, Paul stood for a new theology; the Apocalypse comes nearer to being the prevalent view of the first generation.

In the fourth gospel and the epistles of John we see the future translated into the present tense.   The chief points of primitive eschatology, the antichrist, the parousia, the judgment, the resurrection, are still acknowleged; but there are many antichrists now present; the coming of the Comforter takes the place of the parousia; the judgment takes place when men accept or reject the light; the spiritual transformation into eternal life takes place now.   Eschatology is dissolved into Christology; the Kingdom of God gives way to the Church.   It is far more instructive spiritually to see these different views side by side than to see them mangled and forced into conformity.

5. The most troublesome problem at present is to determine what Jesus himself thought about the future. A group of able scholars has put such emphasis on the eschatological sayings of Jesus that he himself has been turned into an apocalyptic enthusiast and the authority of his ethical teaching has been impaired by being yoked

with apocalyptic expectations. This school of thought
has done valuable work, but the future will probably
show that it has overworked its working hypothesis.
Ordinary critical analysis eliminates a good deal of
eschatological material as later accretions. The earliest
of the documentary sources of the gospels, " Q," contains
least.[1]

All human analogies make it certain that his followers
coloured his ideas with their own previous conceptions.
They could not help it. Language is rich on the lower,
and thin on the higher, spiritual levels. Men of high
religious power have often become poetical makers of
language because they had to wrestle with their medium
of expression and coin new figures and terms. They
must use the lower terminology to express the inexpressi-
ble. Their followers, the loyal lower souls, invariably
coarsen and materialize their teachings, taking the
figures for realities and the accidental for the substance.
The more original and spiritual a teacher is, the larger
will be the inevitable ratio of misunderstanding. We
must remember that the sayings of Jesus were repeated
and transmitted orally for years before our earliest documents were written.

We see the whole situation incorrectly when we tacitly
assume that the ideas of Jesus were uniform throughout his teaching ministry. If we take the doctrine of
his real humanity seriously, he was a growing personality, and his ideas were in the making. A man's ideas

[1] Harnack, " Sayings of Jesus," p. 250. " The tendency to exag-
gerate the apocalyptic and eschatological elements in our Lord's
message and to subordinate to this the merely religious and ethical
elements, will ever find its refutation in Q."

are developed by reacting on the ideas of his fellow men by assent or dissent. It is vital to this problem to know in what direction Jesus was working, into apocalypticism or out of it. We can see that he began with a Jewish horizon and broke his way into a world-wide and human world. How about his eschatology? His earliest parables are a decisive answer. He chose that form of teaching because he wanted to veil and yet reveal his polemical departure from current messianic ideas. He took his illustrations from organic life to express the idea of the gradual growth of the Kingdom. He was shaking off catastrophic ideas and substituting developmental ideas. John had put the judgment at the beginning of the Messiah's work; Jesus pushed it over to the end. He had no taste for that part of the Messianic program. In short, apocalypticism was part of the environment in which he began his thinking; it was not his personal product; he was emancipating himself from it. This is essential.

The intellect of Jesus was religious and prophetic; it was not constructed for apocalypticism. It had too many windows. Paul's ethical teaching got its orientation from his eschatology. The ethics of Jesus would have remained the same if the range of time had lengthened before him. His mind did push impetuously forward, but not toward a scheme of distant events, but toward the immediate saving acts of God. To him the Kingdom of God was both future and present. Whoever can harbour that antimony has risen above apocalypticism.

6. The eschatological schemes of primitive Christianity were all based on the supposition that the end would come soon. If Paul expected a longer interval in his later life, it was a matter of years, not of centuries. The actual duration of the present world for nineteen hundred years has disrupted the whole outline. The judgment and the general resurrection of the dead were necessary parts of the Jewish eschatology because the judgment was needed to decide who was to share in the Messianic happiness, and the resurrection enabled the dead to have their part in it. But what is the use of the judgment if the fate of every man is decided at his death and he goes directly to heaven or hell? And why should a Christian of the first century receive his body again at the general resurrection when he has lived in heaven without it for eighteen hundred years?

History is a revelation of God's will. God thinks in action, and speaks in events. His historical realities are a surer word of God than any prophecy. The least of us today knows things which would have revolutionized the eschatology of the apostles. Are we obedient to the revelation of God if we think more of the sprouting grain than of the full ear, and artificially put ourselves back where we do not belong?

7. The early Catholic Church dealt reverently with the primitive eschatology, and yet changed it profoundly. The earthly millennium was very dear to the common people, but the intellectuals and college graduates who had studied Greek philosophy, had no use for it. The Gnostics hated it, and the semi-Gnostic Alexandrian

theology undermined it. What sort of religious ideal was this which pictured fertile fields and vineyards, lots of babies romping, and old men holding on to life for a hundred years? How did that chime with a holy desire for heaven and the "angelic life" of asceticism? Moreover how did the theocratic and fraternal social order pictured in the millennial ideal square with the Roman Empire, the present distribution of property, the eminence of the upper classes, the permanence of church institutions, and the power of the bishops? (Church historians usually dwell on the theological objections to the "carnal" millennial ideas, but fail to see how distasteful the social elements of the millennial ideal must have been to those who controlled the teaching of the Church.) So the millennium was dropped out, while the safer and more distant parts of the Jewish eschatology were retained. Personal immortality, of course, had long ago crowded the racial eschatology aside in point of real interest.

But the most decisive fact in transforming the substance of primitive eschatology was the Church itself. Its future was now the future of Christianity. In Jewish eschatology there was no Church in the picture; only the people. In primitive Christian thought the Church was real, but it was like a temporary house put up to shelter the believers till the Lord came and the real salvation began. But the Parousia did not come, and the temporary shelter grew and grew, and became the main thing. Even if the doctrines of eschatology had been kept unchanged, they would no longer have been the same after the Catholic Church had come on the scene.

The considerations discussed above are necessary, it seems to me, for a proper understanding and valuation of the biblical material in traditional eschatology. A few constructive propositions can now be made about the future of the race.

1. The future development of the race should have a larger place in practical Christian teaching. The great ethical issues of the future lie in this field, and the mind of Christian men and women should be active there. If we can not be guided by moral and spiritual thought, we shall be guided by bitter experience. The Great War is in truth a grim discussion of the future of the race on this planet, but a discussion with both reason and religion left out. We have the amplest warrant for directing the prophetic thought of religious men toward the social and political future of humanity, for all eschatology derived from Hebrew sources dealt with these interests. A stronger emphasis on the future of the race will simply restore the genuinely Christian emphasis. But if Christian teachers are to teach truth about history, they must have truth to teach. If all ministers and Bible School teachers should now suddenly begin to talk on these subjects, the angels above would probably be astonished to see a still thicker vapour of partisan fury and nationalistic egotism rising from all countries.

2. All Christian discussions of the past and the future must be religious, and filled with the consciousness of God in human affairs. God is in history. He has the initiative. Where others see blind forces working dumb agony, we must see moral will working toward re-

demption and education. A religious view of history involves a profound sense of the importance of moral issues in social life. Sin ruins; righteousness establishes, and love consolidates. In the last resort the issues of future history lie in the moral qualities and religious faith of nations. This is the substance of all Hebrew and Christian eschatology.

3. We need a restoration of the millennial hope, which the Catholic Church dropped out of eschatology. It was crude in its form but wholly right in its substance. The duration of a thousand years is a guess and immaterial. All efforts to fix " times and seasons " are futile. But the ideal of a social life in which the law of Christ shall prevail, and in which its prevalence shall result in peace, justice and a glorious blossoming of human life, is a Christian ideal. An outlook toward the future in which the " spiritual life " is saved and the economic life is left unsaved is both unchristian and stupid. If men in the past have given a " carnal " colouring of richness to the millennial hope, let us renounce that part, and leave the ideals of luxury and excess to men of the present capitalistic order. Our chief interest in any millennium is the desire for a social order in which the worth and freedom of every least human being will be honoured and protected; in which the brotherhood of man will be expressed in the common possession of the economic resources of society; and in which the spiritual good of humanity will be set high above the private profit interests of all materialistic groups. We hope for such an order for humanity as we hope for heaven for ourselves.

4. As to the way in which the Christian ideal of society is to come,— we must shift from catastrophe to development. Since the first century the divine Logos has taught us the universality of Law, and we must apply it to the development of the Kingdom of God. It is the untaught and pagan mind which sees God's presence only in miraculous and thundering action; the more Christian our intellect becomes, the more we see God in growth. By insisting on organic development we shall follow the lead of Jesus when, in his parables of the sower and of the seed growing secretly, he tried to educate his disciples away from catastrophes to an understanding of organic growth. We shall also be following the lead of the fourth gospel, which translated the terms of eschatology into the operation of present spiritual forces. We shall be following the lead of the Church in bringing the future hope down from the clouds and identifying it with the Church; except that we do not confine it to the single institution of the Church, but see the coming of the Kingdom of God in all ethical and spiritual progress of mankind. To convert the catastrophic terminology of the old eschatology into developmental terms is another way of expressing faith in the immanence of God and in the presence of Christ. It is more religious to believe in a present than in an absent and future Christ. Jesus saw the Kingdom as present and future. This change from catastrophe to development is the most essential step to enable modern men to appreciate the Christian hope.[1]

---

[1] Pfleiderer, "Grundriss der christlichen Glaubenslehre," § 177, has this fine summary: "The primitive Christian faith in the return of

5. This process will have to utilize all constructive and educational forces in humanity. In our conception of personal regeneration, likewise, we have been compelled to think less of emotional crises and more of religious nurture and education. The coming of the Kingdom of God will be the regeneration of the super-personal life of the race, and will work out a social expression of what was contained in the personality of Christ.

6. The coming of the Kingdom of God will not be by peaceful development only, but by conflict with the Kingdom of Evil. We should estimate the power of sin too lightly if we forecast a smooth road. Nor does the insistence on continuous development eliminate the possibility and value of catastrophes. Political and social revolutions may shake down the fortifications of the Kingdom of Evil in a day. The Great War is a catastrophic stage in the coming of the Kingdom of God. Its direct effects will operate for generations. Our descendants will have a better perspective than we to see how all the sins of modern civilization have brought forth death after their own kind, and how the social repentance of nations may lay the foundation for a new beginning.

Christ and the establishment of his Kingdom on earth embodied the ideal of an earthly realization of the Kingdom of God. It set up the extensive and intensive penetration of humanity by the Christian spirit as the aim and task of history. The victorious coming and kingly rule of Christ on earth is achieved by the organization of all mankind in a fellowship of children of God, and by the continuous ethical transformation of all society through the power of the Christian spirit. But since this takes place within the historic life of nations, the process is bound to human conditions and limits."

7. An eschatology which is expressed in terms of historic development has no final consummation. Its consummations are always the basis for further development. The Kingdom of God is always coming, but we can never say "Lo here." Theologians often assert that this would be unsatisfactory. "A kingdom of social righteousness can never be perfect; man remains flesh; new generations would have to be trained anew; only by a world-catastrophe can the Kingdom of glory be realized." Apparently we have to postulate a static condition in order to give our minds a rest; an endless perspective of development is too taxing. Fortunately God is not tired as easily as we. If he called humanity to a halt in a "kingdom of glory," he would have on his hands some millions of eager spirits whom he has himself trained to ceaseless aspiration and achievement, and they would be dying of ennui. Besides, what is the use of a perfect ideal which never happens? A progressive Kingdom of righteousness happens all the time in instalments, like our own sanctification. Our race will come to an end in due time; the astronomical clock is already ticking which will ring in the end. Meanwhile we are on the march toward the Kingdom of God, and getting our reward by every fractional realization of it which makes us hungry for more. A stationary humanity would be a dead humanity. The life of the race is in its growth.

Since at death we emigrate from the social life of mankind, the future life of the individual might seem to lie outside of the scope of our discussion. But in truth our conceptions of the life hereafter are deeply affected by the fundamental convictions of the social gospel.

1. There is no inherent contradiction whatever between the hope of the progressive development of mankind toward the Kingdom of God and the hope of the consummation of our personal life in an existence after death. The religious belief in the future life is often bitterly attacked by social radicals because in actual practice the deep interest in it which is cultivated by the Church, weakens interest in social justice and acts as a narcotic to numb the sense of wrong. The more the social gospel does its work within the Church, the more will this moral suspicion against the doctrine of the future life lessen.

2. Belief in a future life is not essential to religious faith. The religious minds who speak to us from the pages of the Old Testament, though they probably believed in future existence, apparently gained neither comfort nor incentive from that belief. There is doubtless an increasing number of religious men and women today who find their satisfaction in serving God now, but expect their personal existence to end at death.

The hope that we shall survive death is not a self-evident proposition. When it is intelligent, it is an act of faith,— a tremendous assertion of faith. It may get support from science, from philosophy, or from psychical research, but its main supports are the resurrection of Christ, his teachings, and the common faith of the Christian Church, which all embolden the individual. Further, the sense of personality, which is intensified and ennobled by the Christian life, and rises to the sense of imperishable worth in the assurance that we are children of God.

3. The hope of a higher life for the race does not solve the problem of the individual. It is a matter of profound satisfaction to those whose life has really matured and been effective to think that they have made a contribution to the richness and the redemption of the race. But none of us lives out his life fully. There are endowments in us which have never been put to use for others, and tastes and cravings which have been starved and suppressed. Moreover only a small percentage of men and women under present conditions are able to develop their powers beyond the feeblest beginnings. A large percentage die in childhood; uncounted others have been used up by labour,— shrunken and intimidated souls. Where do they come in? Is it enough for them to think that they have been laid like sills in the mud that future generations may live in the mansion erected on their dead bodies and souls? Besides, the best society on earth can not last for ever. This planet may end at any time and it is sure to die by collision or old age some time. What then will be the net product of all our labours? Plainly a man has a larger and completer hope if he looks forward to eternal life for himself as well as to a better destiny for the race.

4. It is our business, however, to christianize both expectations. It is possible to fear hell and desire heaven in a pagan spirit, with a narrow-minded selfishness that cares nothing for others, and is simply an extension to the future life of the grabbing spirit fos-

tered by the Kingdom of Evil.   The desire for heaven gets Christian dignity and quality only when it arises on the basis of that solidaristic state of mind which is cultivated by the social gospel.

5. Two theories, quite unlike, are held as private opinions by many Christian individuals, though not sanctioned by traditional theology.   The theory of conditional immortality is largely based on evolutionary ideas.   It holds that only those will survive who have attained to a spiritual life capable of surviving.   The theory of re-incarnation, which has been held by a few eminent minds in theology and by many outside of it, comes to us mostly through theosophical channels from the East.   It teaches that we live in a succession of lives, each of them adapted to the spiritual attainments of the individual and disciplinary in its effect; through them we can gradually exhaust the possibilities of human life and rise to spiritual levels above man.

The social gospel could utilize the latter idea if it were commonly held.   It would be an attractive idea to those who have fought for humanity, to come back to this earth and help on the Cause once more, beginning afresh on the basis of the experiences and character attained in the present life.   The reward of a fine life, then, would be more life of the same kind.   On the other hand there would be remarkable chances of retribution and purgation.   A man who has prostituted women, might be re-incarnated as a prostitute and see how he likes it.   A woman who has lived softly on the proceeds of child labour might be re-born as a little

Georgia girl working in a cotton mill. A man who has helped to lynch a negro, might be born in a black skin and be lynched by his own grandsons.

Both theories, however, are somewhat aristocratic in their effect. When we consider the terrible inequality of opportunity for spiritual development in our present world, it does not convey a sense of Christian solidarity to think of a minority climbing into eternal life while the majority wilt away like unfertilized blossoms.

The theory of re-incarnation seems to offer a fair chance for all, provided each soul is really started in the exact environment which it has earned by its past life and in which it can best develop for the future. Theosophists have devised a spiritual bureaucracy of "Masters" or higher spiritual beings who manage this very essential matter. In actual practice it is interesting to observe that those who profess to have a recollection of past existences, all seem to have been stately and famous personages. They do sometimes become savages or courtesans for one life-time to expiate dark deeds of vengeance, or as interesting slumming expeditions. The plain people who just raise hogs or sell cheese in one existence, seem to forget it in the next, which is very human.

It is a more serious question whether this doctrine is not incompatible with social unrest and indignation. If the poor are in their present condition because they have deserved it in a previous life, why should we worry about them? The present child-labourers may be former stock-holders who have come back to get the other side, and we should be interfering with justice by trying to uplift them. If people living in bad tenements are in the conditions best adapted to their future spiritual development in later incarnations, we may be tampering with things too high for us in condemning the tenements. This doctrine explains the present inequalities too well. It seems to cut the nerve of the social movement much more effectively than the hope of heaven ever did.

Of course the Christian realm of grace would disappear, and a reign of Karma and exact retribution would supplant it.

6. The most unattractive element in the orthodox outlook on the future life is the immediate fixity of the two states. When we die, our destiny is immediately and irrevocably settled for us. As the Westminster Larger Catechism (Question 86) has it:

> The communion in glory with Christ, which the members of the invisible church enjoy immediately after death, is in that their souls are then made perfect in holiness and received into the highest heavens, where they behold the face of God in light and glory; waiting for the full redemption of their bodies, which even in death continue united to Christ, and rest in their graves as in beds, till at the last day they be again united to their souls. Whereas the souls of the wicked are at their death cast into hell, where they remain in torments and utter darkness; and their bodies kept in their graves, as in their prisons, until the resurrection and judgment of the great day.

This belief was novel at the time of the Reformation, and the precision and emphasis of this statement are directed against the idea of purgatory. The idea of a fixed condition is so unlike any life we know and so contradictory of our aspirations that our imagination stands still before a tedious sameness of bliss. The rich diversification in Dante shows the possibility of the other view.[1] We want the possibility of growth. We can not conceive of finite existence or of human happiness except in terms of growth. It would be more satisfactory for modern minds and for Christian minds to think of an unlimited scale of ascent toward God, reaching from the lowest to the highest, within which every spirit would hold the place for which it was fitted, and each could advance as it grew. This would satisfy our sense of justice. Believers in the social gospel will probably agree that some people have deserved hell and ought to get theirs. But no man, in any human sense of justice, has deserved an eternity of hell. On the other hand, it jars our sense of justice to see some individuals go to heaven totally exempt. They have given hell to others and ought to have a taste of it somewhere, even if they are regenerate and saved men.

7. This idea would also satisfy our Christian faith in the redeeming mercy of God. In this ascending scale of beings none would be so high that he could not be drawn still closer to God, and none so low that he would be beyond the love of God. God would still be teaching and saving all. If we learned in heaven that a minority were in hell, we should look at God to see what he was going to do about it; and if he did nothing, we should look at Jesus to see how this harmonized with what he taught us about his Father; and if he did nothing, something would die out of heaven. Jonathan Edwards

[1] Prof. William Adams Brown, in the closing pages of his "Christian Theology in Outline," points out the need for progress, and explains the hold which the doctrine of purgatory has on Catholics.

demanded that we should rejoice in the damnation of
those whom the sovereign election of God abandoned to
everlasting torment. Very justly, for we ought to be
able to rejoice in what God does. But we can not rejoice
in hell. It can't be done. At least by Christians. The
more Christian Christ has made a soul, the more it
would mourn for the lost brothers. The conception of
a permanent hell was tolerable only while God was conceived as an autocratic sovereign dealing with his subjects; it becomes intolerable when the Father deals with
his children.

To-day many Protestants are allowing the physical
fires of hell to go out, and make the pain of hell to
consist in the separation from God. They base the
continuance of hell, not on the sovereign decree of God
but on the progressive power of sin which gradually ex-
tinguishes all love of good and therewith all capacity
for salvation. But this remains to be proven. Who
has ever met a man that had no soft spot of tenderness,
no homesick yearning after uprightness left in him? If
God has not locked the door of hell from the outside,
but men remain in it because they prefer the darkness,
then there is bound to be a Christian invasion of hell.
All the most Christian souls in heaven would get down
there and share the life of the wicked, in the high hope
that after all some scintilla of heavenly fire was still
smouldering and could be fanned into life. And they
would be headed by Him who could not stand it to think
of ninety-nine saved and one caught among the thorns.

The idea of two fixed groups does not satisfy any real
requirement. Men justly feared the earlier Universal-

ist doctrine that all men enter salvation at death. That took sin lightly and offended the sense of justice. The idea of a scale of life in which each would be as far from God and in as much darkness and narrowness as he deserved, would constitute a grave admonition to every soul. Indeed it would contain more summons to self-discipline than the present idea that as long as a man is saved at all, he is saved completely and escapes all consequences. To-day the belief in hell has weakened in great numbers of people, and in that case there is no element of fear at all to aid men in self-control. The Christian idea would have to combine the just effects of sin for all and the operation of saving mercy on all.

8. Our personal eschatology is characterized by an unsocial individualism. In the present life we are bound up with wife and children, with friends and work-mates, in a warm organism of complex life. When we die, we join — what? A throng of souls, an unorganized crowd of saints, who each carry a harp and have not even organized an orchestra. The question is even debated whether we shall know each other in heaven, and whether we shall remember and have a sense of our identity. What satisfaction would there be in talking to Isaiah or Paul if they could not remember what books they wrote and at last set our minds at rest on those questions of criticism? Anyone trained in the mind of Christ by the social gospel wants organic relations of duty and friendship. How can we become more Christ-like on earth or in heaven except by love and service? The chief effort of the Holy Spirit in our earthly life

was to develop our capacity for love and our sense of
solidarity and responsibility.   Is this training to go for
nothing in heaven, or is this present life the real preparation for the kind of life we are to live there, and the
basis for promotion and growth?   If the future life is to
be the consummation of all that is good and divine here,
it must offer fellowship with God and man.   This is the
point to be insisted on in our popular teaching, and not
the painlessness and the eternal rest.

9. And how about labour and service?   Is not our
heaven too much a heaven of idleness?   It looks as if it
had been conceived by oppressed and exploited people
who regarded labour as a curse and wanted a rest more
than anything else.   The social gospel wants to see all
men on earth at productive work, but none doing too
much of it.   It carries that expectation into the idea of
heaven.   Dr. William N. Clarke, who was a most loving
heart and had no child of his own, makes the point in
his "Outline of Christian Theology" (pp. 419–20)
that a third part of humanity dies in childhood, with
undeveloped personality.   "This significant fact has
never yet been admitted to the popular thought of the
future life, or exerted its due influence in theology."   If
these youthful spirits are to grow and develop, they
must live a life of free and responsible action.   If the
children in heaven need education and care, "opportunities of usefulness and help must open in inexhaustible
abundance to those who are farther advanced in holy
experience, and the heavenly life must be intensely active
and interesting."   Dr. Clarke thought this was "a vast
enrichment of our ideas of the other world."

This is a thought worthy of a man who followed a Master that gathered the children to his heart. The social gospel would add the kindred fact that a further large proportion of individuals are left so underdeveloped by our earthly social system that they deserve a heavenly post-graduate course to make it up to them. It would be a great joy in heaven to find men trooping in from mines and shops, and women from restaurant kitchens and steaming laundries, and getting their long delayed college education.

This suggests another form of service. We are all conscious of having failed in some of our human relations, giving indifference instead of sympathy, idleness instead of service, laying our burdens on others without lending a hand with theirs. Some have done little in the sum total of their life except to add to the weight on others, and monopolizing the opportunities which ought to have been shared by many. The future life offers a chance for reparation, not by way of kindness but of justice. Suppose that a stockholder has taken large dividends out of a mill-town, leaving only the bare minimum to the workers, and stripping their lives of what could humanize them. He followed the custom of his day, and the point of view of his social class hid the injustice from his conscience. But in the other world he sees things differently and becomes a belated convert to the social gospel. About him are the men and women whose souls he has starved. Would not justice demand that he remain on the lower levels of life with them until he was able to take upward with him all whom he had retarded? Suppose that a man sent a

child into life without accepting the duties of fatherhood, breaking the spirit of a girl and her family, and
leaving his child to be submerged in poverty and vice.
Would it not be just and Christian to require that he
serve the soul of his child until it is what it might have
been? Such labour and expiation might well keep us
busy for some part of eternity, and in doing it, relation-
ships of love and service would be formed which would
make us fit to live closer to the Source of Love.

Of course some of the ideas I have ventured to put
down are simply the play of personal fancy about a
fascinating subject. There are only a few things which
we can claim with any assurance, and these are not based
on a single prediction, or on some passage, the origin or
meaning of which may be disputed, but on the substance
of the gospel of Christ. These are: that the love of God
will go out forever to his children, and especially to the
neediest, drawing them to him and, where necessary,
saving them; that personality energized by God is ever
growing; that the law of love and solidarity will be even
more effective in heaven than on earth; and that salvation, growth, and solidarity are conditioned on inter-
change of service.

The worth of personality, freedom, growth, love,
solidarity, service,— these are marks of the Kingdom of
God. In Christ's thought the Kingdom of God was to
come from heaven to earth, so that God's will would be
done on earth as it is in heaven. So then it exists in
heaven; it is to be created on earth. All true joys on
earth come from partial realizations of the Kingdom of

God; the joy that awaits us will consist in living within the full realization of the Kingdom. Our labour for the Kingdom here will be our preparation for our participation hereafter. The degree in which we have absorbed the laws of the Kingdom into our character will determine our qualification for the life of heaven. If in any respect we have not been saved from the Kingdom of Evil, we shall be aliens and beginners in the Kingdom of God. Thus heaven and earth are to be parts of the same realm. Spiritual influences come to us; spiritual personalities go out from us. When our life is in God it has continuity.

CHAPTER XIX

THE SOCIAL GOSPEL AND THE ATONEMENT

To countless Christian minds the doctrine of the atonement has been the marrow of theology. We have reserved it for the close of our discussion. Does the social gospel contain anything which would verify, interpret, quicken, or expand that doctrine? And what form of the doctrine would best express and support the social gospel?

The theological interpretation of the death of Christ has a long and varied history. It will aid us in estimating our modern needs if we pass it briefly in review.

To the first disciples the death of their Lord was an astonishing catastrophe, an unexpected, terrible, and apparently impossible outcome of the work of the Messiah. For that very reason they craved an explanation of the event which would interpret it as a fundamental part of God's plan. Their method was to prove that it had been foretold throughout the Scripture and foreshadowed by typology. Paul was the first to give the death of our Lord a really central position in a theological system.

But the early Church never appropriated or utilized more than a few leading ideas of Paul. The most popular and elaborate theological explanation was the theory that Christ's death was a ransom paid to Satan. By the fall the human race became subject to Satan, and he had a rightful claim on it as its sovereign. God in mercy desired to emancipate humanity from the thraldom of Satan, but would not use his superior power to wrest from him what was his by legal right. So he offered Christ to Satan as a ransom in exchange, and Satan gladly accepted. But in killing the sinless Christ, Satan overstepped his legal claims and thereby forfeited all his rights. Or, according to other Fathers, Satan was attracted by the human beauty of Christ, but did not realize that this was the incarnate Logos; the marriage of Mary to Joseph had concealed from him the mystery of the incarnation. God knew beforehand that even if Satan took possession of the ransom, he could never hold Christ. So God offered Satan a bait and tricked him. When Satan tried to imprison Christ in Hades, he burst the gates and came forth with a throng of souls. This legal negotiation between two sovereigns reminds one of modern diplomacy. A few Fathers objected to the element of trickery, but on the whole this was the orthodox theology till Anselm of Canterbury substituted something better for it in A. D. 1098.

Anselm's doctrine was a real advance in ethical and religious insight. Its main points are these: Our sin has robbed God of the honour due him; an equivalent must be offered him before he can forgive sin; we ourselves can not render the "satisfaction" due to him; God alone can; therefore God had to become man; being divine and sinless, his death furnished an offset and equivalent for the boundless sins of mankind.

This theory has furnished the ground-work for orthodox theology ever since Anselm. Yet it raises unanswer-

able questions and in some respects offends our Christian
convictions. How can it satisfy justice to have an innocent one die in place of the guilty? How can God pay
an equivalent to himself? If the debt due to God has
been paid by the death of Christ, why is it any longer an
act of grace on the part of God to remit sin? The debt
we owe to God is not a financial but a moral debt; another man may discharge a debt of $100 for me, but no
man can discharge my obligations as a son or as a father
for me; how then can the debt we owe to God be paid
by another? If Christ fulfilled the law for us, why are
we still obliged to fulfil it? These questions shock our
Christian feeling. This is where we get when we try to
formulate the relations between God and us on the basis
of law and in forensic terms. It ends in wiping out the
love and mercy of God, our most essential Christian
conviction.

The Reformation made no essential change in this doctrine. Lutherans and Calvinists on the whole taught
the same outline of atonement. God, in mercy toward
fallen humanity, sent his Son, who shared both the divine and human nature, in order to redeem and recon-
cile. The justice of God demands the condemnation of
all. God can exercise mercy only if vicarious satisfaction
is rendered. The infinite worth of the divine nature in
Christ makes his suffering an equivalent for the infinite
sins of mankind. Christ experienced the wrath of God
in his suffering, and that wrath is now satisfied, so that
God can forgive.

These traditional theological explanations of the death
of Christ have less biblical authority than we are ac-

customed to suppose. The fundamental terms and ideas —" satisfaction," " substitution," " imputation," " merit "— are post-biblical ideas, and are alien from the spirit of the gospel.

It is important to note that every theory of the atonement necessarily used terms and analogies taken from the social life of that age, and that the spirit and problems of contemporary life are always silent factors in the construction of theory.   The early Church set the model of formulating the doctrine in the terminology of sacrifice. To us sacrificing is a matter of antiquarian knowledge, kept alive mainly by the Bible.   To Christians of the first three centuries it was a social institution which they saw in operation all about them.   Paul saw in the death of Christ the solution of the great social problem of his life, the abolition of the Jewish Law and the emancipation of Gentile missions.   The theory that the death of Christ was a ransom to Satan was the outgrowth of the semi-dualistic religion of the Empire and the prevalent belief in the rule of demons.   Anselm's theory seems to me clearly the product of the penitential practices of the medieval Church, within which Anselm lived and moved and which was his social order.   Every priest in the confessional was constantly assessing the delinquencies of men in terms of penalty and merit, and assigning so much inconvenience or suffering as a " satisfaction " for so much sin.   Perhaps the commercial and governmental theories of later Protestantism were the natural social product of the age of capitalistic merchants and of limited monarchies.

These social realities which lay back of the theories gave them their influence and convincing power at the time they originated and for a long time thereafter, but when these social realities disappear, the theories of the atonement based on them become artificial and unconvincing, and sometimes repulsive. Analogies and illustrations taken from the priestly slaughtering of animals or the ritual functions of the Jewish high-priest are remote from our imagination, and instead of clarifying the facts, they themselves need elaborate explanation. Forensic methods and the dealings of autocratic rulers arouse our moral antagonism and have brought the teachings about the atonement under suspicion.

Our dominant ideas are personality and social solidarity. The problems which burden us are the social problems. Has the death of Christ any relation to these? Have we not just as much right to connect this supreme religious event with our problems as Paul and Anselm and Calvin, and to use the terminology and methods of our day? In so far as the historical and social sciences have taught our generation to comprehend solidaristic facts, we are in a better situation to understand the atonement than any previous generation.

As Christian men we believe that the death of our Lord concerns us all. Our sins caused it. He bore the sin of the world. In turn his death was somehow for our good. Our spiritual situation is fundamentally changed in consequence of it. But how? How did he bear our sins? How did his death affect God? How did it affect us? These three questions we shall discuss.

How did Jesus bear sins which he did not commit?

The old theology replied, by imputation. But guilt and merit are personal. They can not be transferred from one person to another. We tamper with moral truth when we shuffle them about. Imputation is a legal device to enable the law to hold one man responsible for the crime committed by another. Imputation sees mankind as a mass of individuals, and the debts of every individual are transferred to Christ. The solution does not lie in that way.

Neither is it enough to say that Jesus bore our sins by sympathy. His contact with sin was a matter of experience as well as sympathy, and experience cuts deeper. Child-birth and travail reveal the realities of life to a woman more than sympathetic observation.

How did Jesus bear our sins? The bar to a true understanding of the atonement has been our individualism. The solution of the problem lies in the recognition of solidarity.

By his human life Jesus was bound up backward and forward and sideward with the life of humanity. He received the influences of the historical life of the Jewish people through the channels of social tradition, and he transmitted the effects of his own life and personality to the future through the same channels. Palestine was only a little corner of the Roman Empire, but the full life of humanity was there, just as a man's little finger is filled with the flow of life which nourishes his whole body. Even the feeblest mind has some consciousness of the tide of life playing about him. The stronger and more universal a human personality is, the more will he

consciously absorb the general life and identify himself
with it.   To a genius, or to one whose social feeling is
made vivid and sensitive by love, even small experiences
unlock life, and from a small circle one may prolong great
sectors into the wider concentric circles.   Jesus had an
unparalleled sense of solidarity.   Thereby he had the
capacity to generalize his personal experiences and make
them significant of the common life.

Now, this race life of ours is pervaded by sin; not only
by sporadic acts of folly, waywardness, vice or crime
which spring spontaneously from human life, but by
organized forces and institutions of evil which have
stabilized the power of sin and made it effective.   Our
analysis of race sin culminated in the recognition of a
Kingdom of Evil (Chapter IX).   Jesus lived in the midst
of that Kingdom, and it was this which killed him.

Every personal act of sin, however isolated it may
seem, is connected with racial sin.   Evil social customs
and ideas stimulate or facilitate it; in turn it strengthens
the social suggestion to evil for others.

But personal transgression does not develop moral
force and resentment enough to slay the prophets of
God.   It takes public and organized evil to do that.
When a travelling pedlar cheats a farmer's wife, he is
part and parcel of an ancient system of business which
overreaches the customer if it can.   But if the pedlar
learns that a socialist editor is advocating a system of
production which would abolish him and his cunning, he
does not waylay and kill the editor to stop his pen.   On
the other hand if trade and finance have developed a
lucrative system of evil income, such as the American

slave trade, or the English opium trade, or the universal liquor traffic, or Five Power Loans to China, or a monopoly of colonial trade, then it will resist interference. The gigantic collective pedlar will blast reputations by the press he controls, break men financially by the bank credit he controls, or ruin men politically by the party machinery or official power he controls. When Evil is organized, the prophets suffer. There is probably not a single State of our Union which has not seen the reputation and financial or political standing of good men killed in cold blood because they sincerely opposed high class graft.

These public evils so pervade the social life of humanity in all times and all places that no one can share the common life of our race without coming under the effect of these collective sins. He will either sin by consenting in them, or he will suffer by resisting them. Jesus did not in any real sense bear the sin of some ancient Briton who beat up his wife in B. C. 56, or of some mountaineer in Tennessee who got drunk in A. D. 1917. But he did in a very real sense bear the weight of the public sins of organized society, and they in turn are causally connected with all private sins.

As one looks across human history with a mind enlightened by the thought of the Kingdom of God, he sees a few great permanent evils which have blighted the life of the race and of every individual in it. They always change their form and yet remain the same in substance. Seize and fight the power of evil at any point, as you will, and soon one of these ruling evils will lift its head and

strike back at you.   The stronger and more influential
a man's life is, and the broader his moral interests, the
deeper will be his experience of these chief evils.   I have
been impressed with the fact that so many of them
plainly converged on Jesus and had a part in doing him to
death.

These evils were not as gigantic and fully developed in
Palestine as they have been in the great Empires, including our own.   But the fact that even in this remote corner of the ancient world they were present and virulent,
proves their universal power in the life of the race.
There are few communities, a cross-section of which
would not reveal their presence.   Jesus experienced his
full collision with them when he came to the capital of
his nation in the last week.   There is a reason why
prophets are most likely to die at Jerusalem.

To make this clear I shall enumerate six sins, all of a
public nature, which combined to kill Jesus.   He bore
their crushing attack in his body and soul.   He bore
them, not by sympathy, but by direct experience.   In so
far as the personal sins of men have contributed to the
existence of these public sins, he came into collision with
the totality of evil in mankind.   It requires no legal fic-
tion of imputation to explain that " he was wounded for
our transgressions, he was bruised for our iniquities."
Solidarity explains it.

The most persistent force which pushed Jesus toward
death, the earliest on the field and the latest on the watch,
was religious bigotry.   At that time it was embodied in
the intellectual expounders and the devotees of Judaism

rather than in the priests.   Jesus acknowledged the earnestness and outward rectitude of his opponents.   The traditional zeal of Judaism, the solemn injunctions of their most sacred books, and the punishments the nation had incurred by slackness and tolerance in the past, seemed ample justification of the vigor with which they set themselves against a man who seemed to flout the Sabbath, to disregard the laws of fasting, to eat with profane and unwashed hands, to overthrow the entire doctrine of clean and unclean food, and to confuse all moral distinctions between good and bad by associating with irreligious men.   He was suspected of far-reaching designs against the religion of Jehovah; he had offered to substitute a temple not made with hands for their ancestral sanctuary.

So they counteracted him by innuendo and direct charges, and tried to entrap him.   The great invective of Jesus shows that he regarded their influence as the chief cause for the frustration of his work.   They were the active agents in the legal steps which led to his death and exerted the pressure to which Pilate had to yield.   Secular governors are but poor persecutors compared with men of religion.   The persecutions of the Roman Empire against Christians were feeble and occasional as compared with the zeal of the Inquisition.   It takes religion to put a steel edge on social intolerance.   Just because it is so high and its command of social loyalty so great, it is pitiless when it goes wrong.

Religious bigotry has been one of the permanent evils of mankind, the cause of untold social division, bitterness, persecution, and religious wars.   It is always a social sin.

Estimate the harm which the exponents of religion have done simply by suppressing the prophetic minds who had received from God fresh thought on spiritual and intellectual problems, and by cowing those who might have followed the prophets.

Jesus was killed by ecclesiastical religion. He might have appeared in almost any highly developed nation and suffered the same fate. Certainly after religion bore his name, there were a thousand situations in which he would have been put to death by those who offered salvation in his name. Innumerable individuals contribute their little quota to make up this collective evil, and when once the common mind is charged with it, it gets innumerable outlets. This sin, then, was borne by Jesus, not by imputation, nor by sympathy, but by direct experience.

A second social evil which contributed to kill him was the combination of graft and political power. Those who are in control of the machinery of organized society are able to use it for selfish and predatory ends, turning into private profit what ought to serve the common good. In the Oberammergau Passion Play the whole plot turns on the cleansing of the temple. This interpretation has found scholarly support. The market was originally outside the temple gates. A location inside would be a trading privilege. Did the pious hierarchy take no offence at the chaffering and dickering inside of the sacred enclosure? Or was somebody making something out of it? Knowing what we do of human nature and the versatility of graft, it does not seem likely that the concessionaires got their inside stands for love. If this conjecture is true, the feeling that the Galilæan prophet was on the side of right would explain the ready yielding to his command; and the active concern of the traders and the hierarchy in their common business would explain the energy with which the hostile action henceforward moved against him.

We are on sure ground when we realize that the prophetic leadership of Jesus endangered the power of the ruling class. There is always an oligarchy, wherever you look; monarchial and republican forms of government are both protective devices for the-group-that-controls-things. This group is the universal government. For every oligarchy political power is convertible into financial income and social influence, thus satisfying the powerful double instinct for money and for power.

In the case of the Jewish people, the Romans held the chief power and collected the main taxes through the concessionaires called the publicani or publicans. But considerable powers were left to the native oligarchy, especially the control of the institutions of religion, and from the loyalty of the Jews to their ancestral and centralized faith a modest income in cash and considerable social prestige could be harvested. Even distant colonies in the pagan cities remitted the annual temple tax, and a poor widow dropped her two farthings. Also it was pleasant to be called Rabbi, and to get the best seats in the synagogue. Their sincere concern for their religion was reinforced by concern for their special privileges as the custodians of the religious institutions and jurisdictions.

Jesus was a prophet of religion; they were exploiters of religion. This added durable fuel to their bigotry. They assumed that Jesus planned to stir up the revolutionary elements, and they feared that a messianic revolt would lose them the remnants of their power. "Whatever is to be done?" the fourth gospel reports them as saying; "if we let him alone like this, everybody will believe in him, and then the Romans will come and suppress our holy Place and our nation." Caiaphas formulated the situation with Machiavellian frankness: "You know nothing about it. You do not understand it is in your interest that one man should die for the People instead of the whole nation being destroyed." [1]

A third historic evil is the corruption of justice. We remember how often the Hebrew prophets denounced the judges who took bribes against the poor. Bearing false witness was so constant an evil that it got a place in the decalogue. Jesus took an illustration of the power of prayer from the case of a widow and a hard judge; though the judge cared neither for religion nor public opinion, she got the better of him by sheer feminine persistence. But it was hard for widows who had no pull.

Injustice between man and man is inevitable and bad enough. But it is far worse when the social institution set up in the name of justice gives its support to injustice. What nation can claim to be free from this? We have thought of the political prisons of autocratic Russia as a remnant of the dark ages, but the War has shown that even in free countries the judicial process can swiftly

[1] John xi, 47–50.

break conscientious convictions and the most cherished rights of democracy. In our own country the delays and appeals permitted by our legal procedure set up a terrible inequality between the rich and poor. Years of public agitation have produced no adequate change. Even if the judge is wholly free from bias, the law itself in all countries, presumably, is on the side of property. The British Parliament, "the mother of free institutions," has always been an assembly of propertied men; only in recent years has it contained an efficient minority of representatives of the working class. Our own legislatures rarely contain any spokesman of the class which needs a voice most of all.

As soon as Jesus was arrested, he became a victim of the courts. In the ecclesiastical court, we are told, distorted and bribed testimony was used. His followers were not present and we have no report of eye-witnesses. It may be that he never made the claim that he would come as the apocalyptic Messiah, and that it was concocted in order to have a political charge to present in the Roman court. The priestly court condemned him on a priestly charge; he was a heretic and blasphemer.

In the Roman court the pull of the upper classes and the pressure of mob clamour were allowed to influence judicial procedure. It was Pilate's high privilege to protect a man whom he felt to be innocent; he had the military power of Rome to back his verdict. He yielded to pressure because his own career, as we know from secular history, was corrupt; the Jews threatened to "get him," and he knew they could. So he took some water and demonstratively washed his hands of what he yet

consented to do. Pilate's wash-bowl deserves to be a
mystic symbol, the counter-part of the Holy Grail.

So Jesus made experience of one of the permanent sins
of organized society, bearing in his own body and soul
what so many thousands of the poor and weak have borne
before and after, the corruption of justice.

A fourth permanent social sin which participated in
the death of Jesus was the mob spirit and mob action.
The mob spirit is the social spirit gone mad.   The social
group then escapes from the control of its wiser and
fairer habits, and is lashed into action by primitive pas-
sions.   The social spirit reacts so powerfully on individuals, that when once the restraints of self-criticism and
self-control are shot back, the crowd gets drunk on the
mere effluvia of its own emotions.   We know only too
well that a city of respectable and religious people will
do fiendish acts of cruelty and obscenity.

There are radical mobs and conservative mobs.   Well-
dressed mobs are more dangerous than ragged mobs
because they are far more efficient.   Entire nations may
come under the mob spirit, and abdicate their judgment.

Rarely are mobs wholly spontaneous; usually there is
leadership to fanaticize the masses.   At this point this
sin connects with the sins of selfish leadership which we
have analysed before.   Sometimes the crowd turns
against the oligarchy; usually the oligarchy manipulates
the crowd.

So it was in the case of Jesus.   The mob shouted for
the physical force man and against the man who embodied
the better spirit of the Jewish nation.   There was " pa-

triotism " in this choice.   Pilate realized that, and tried
to play on it by calling Jesus the king of the Jews, but the
native politicians outplayed him.   The choice was prophetic.   It was the Barabbas type which led the nation
to its doom in the Jewish War and the later risings of the
Jewish patriots.

So this pervasive sin of community life, the intoxication of the social spirit, before which so many prophets
and semi-prophets have had to quail, contributed to the
death of Jesus.   He bore it, not by sympathy or imputation, but by experience.

The fifth universal sin of organized society which co-
operated in the death of Christ was militarism.   So far
as we know, Jesus never passed through an actual war.
He probably never saw his home burned, his father killed,
his sisters ravished, nor was he ever forced to bear arms.
But that he had convictions on war is plain from his sayings.   " He that taketh the sword shall perish by the
sword," shows clear comprehension of the fact that in
war neither side gains, and that the reactions of war are
as dangerous as the direct effects; of which fact ample
demonstrations are before us.

If the words spoken in his lament over Jerusalem are
authentic, he not only foresaw that the present drift
would carry his nation to war and destruction, but he
regarded the acceptance of his leadership as the one
means by which his people might have escaped their
doom: " If thou hadst known in this day the things that
make for peace!   But now they are hidden from thine
eyes."   To his mind, then, the Kingdom of God must

have had a conscious and definite relation to war and force revolution.

With his arrest Jesus fell into the hands of the war system. When the soldiers stripped him, beat his back with the leaded whip, pressed the wreath of thorns into his scalp, draped a purple mantle around him and saluted this amusing king of the Jews, and when they blindfolded and struck him, asking him to prophesy who it was and spitting in his face,— this was the humour of the barrack room. This was fun as the professional soldiers of the Roman Empire saw it. The men who drove the spikes through his hands and feet were the equivalent of a firing-squad told off for duty at an execution, and when they gambled for his clothes, they were taking their soldiers' perquisites.

The last of this group of racial sins is class contempt. Class pride and its obverse passion, class contempt, are the necessary spiritual product of class divisions. They are the direct negation of solidarity and love. They substitute a semi-human, semi-ethical relation for full human fraternity. The class system, therefore, is a sinful denial of the Kingdom of God, and one of the characteristic marks and forces of the Kingdom of Evil.

It is almost universal. Our capitalistic semi-democracy has alleviated it but not overcome it. Indeed, while some other nations are slowly breaking up the class systems erected in the past, the present economic tendencies in our country, if allowed to go on, will inevitably build up a durable class system. Economic facts mock at political theory. Sixty-five per cent of the national property before the war was held by two per cent of the population. The war has contributed enormously to the aggregation of great fortunes. [1] Parasitic incomes produce class differences; class differences create class pride and class contempt.

This sin has always rested heavily on the great mass of mankind. It expresses itself in social customs and in the laws of a nation. Where an aristocracy exists, either its members are formally exempt from the degrading forms of punishment, as in Russia, or they are ostensibly liable to them but practically exempt by the inability to put them in prison or keep them there.

In Roman law crucifixion was a punishment reserved for offenders of the lowest classes. No Roman citizen could be crucified. Cicero flung it at Verres as a culminating accusation in the counts of his misrule that he had crucified a Roman. When Jesus was nailed to the tree, therefore, he bore not only the lightning shoots of physical pain imposed by the cruelties of criminal law, but also that contempt for the lower classes which has always dehumanized the upper classes, numbed and crippled the spiritual self-respect of the lower classes, and set up insuperable barriers to the spirit of the Kingdom of God.

Religious bigotry, the combination of graft and political power, the corruption of justice, the mob spirit, mili-

[1] The Minority Report of the Senate Committee on Finance, August 13, 1917, contains tables of 95 industrial corporations and 50 railways in which the average income of 1911–13 is deducted from the net income of 1916, leaving special war profits of 100%, 400%, 1400%, 4500% in some cases. Thus the Bethlehem Steel Corporation made over 1300% or $40,518,860, and the Du Pont Powder Co. over 1400% or $76,581,729.

tarism, and class contempt,— every student of history will recognize that these sum up constitutional forces in the Kingdom of Evil.   Jesus bore these sins in no legal or artificial sense, but in their impact on his own body and soul.   He had not contributed to them, as we have, and yet they were laid on him.   They were not only the sins of Caiaphas, Pilate, or Judas, but the social sin of all mankind, to which all who ever lived have contributed, and under which all who ever lived have suffered. [1]

The spiritual insight of Jesus himself has added a further step to this solidaristic interpretation of his death. In the parable of the Vineyard he described the religious history of his nation as a continuous struggle, with God and his prophets on one side, and the selfish exploiters of religion on the other, and set his own impending death at the end of the prophetic succession as its culmination. This was an historical, social, and solidaristic interpretation of his death.

At the close of the invective against the religious leaders (Mathew 23) he again outlined this historical process, in which the ruling classes of the past had always silenced the living voices of God, but managed to utilize them

---

[1] I have not seen this analysis attempted before.   My attention has been called to a sermon by President William DeWitt Hyde, on "The Sins which Crucified Jesus," in the collection of "Modern Sermons by World Scholars," Vol. IV, in which he follows a similar line of inquiry. He specifies the envy of the hierarchy, the money-love of Judas, slander, and the servility of Pilate. But, except in the first part, dealing with the hierarchy, he does not place the discussion under the category of solidarity, and that is the decisive point of my argument.   See also Henry Sloane Coffin, "Social Aspects of the Cross."

posthumously among the decorative elements and authorities of religion. He warned his own generation that
they were on the point of repeating this sin by persecuting
the new prophets whom he would send. Thereby they
would prove that they were " the sons of them that slew
the prophets "; they would " fill up the measure of their
fathers "; and would bring upon themselves " all the
righteous blood shed on the earth."

His thought is that by repeating the sins of the past we
are involved in the guilt of the past. We are linked in a
solidarity of evil and guilt with all who have done the
same before us, and all who will do the same after us.
In so far then as we, by our conscious actions or our passive consent, have repeated the sins which killed Jesus,
we have made ourselves guilty of his death. If those
who actually killed him stood before us, we could not
wholly condemn them, but would have to range ourselves
with them as men of their own kind.

This is Christ's own theology. It is not a legal theory
of imputation, but a conception of spiritual solidarity, by
which our own free and personal acts constitute us partakers of the guilt of others.

Along two lines we have replied to the question how the
sins of the world were borne by Jesus: First, the realistic
forces which killed Jesus were not accidental and personal
causes of his death, but were the reaction of the totality of
racial sin against him; and second, the guilt of those who
did it spreads to all who re-affirm the acts which killed
him. The key to the problem is contained in the realization of solidarity.

We have understood only one side of the atonement when we comprehend how the sins of humanity converged in the death of Jesus and were borne by him.   The next question is, in what sense this can be said to affect God and to change the relation of humanity to him.

The first step toward a true view of the atonement is to see the death of Christ as an integral part of his life. Theology has made a fundamental mistake in treating the atonement as something distinct, and making the life of Jesus a mere staging for his death, a matter almost negligible in the work of salvation.

It is not given to all to die a significant death.   Usually, as we age or sicken, the work of our life and the things we have loved and lived for, begin to drop from our hands.   Instead of dying fighting, we die what our pagan forefathers called a " straw-death."   Sometimes a brave life ends in a dishonorable death.   The death of Jesus was wholly of one piece with his life.   He gathered all the radiance of his character and purpose in a focus-point of blazing light, and there he died.

In living his life and dying his death as he did, Jesus lived out, confirmed, and achieved his own personality. He did it for himself, as well as for God and humanity. There was no " merit " in the medieval sense in it; nothing superfluous which he could hand over and credit to others to make up their defects.   Just as we owe God the complete best that is in us, so Jesus too owed life and death to God.   He was under the law he had proclaimed, that " from him to whom much is given, much shall be required."

His death was not simply an infliction from without.

He accepted his suffering not as a fate to be warded off, but with inward assent and acceptance. He knew it was coming.. "I must go on my way to-day and to-morrow and the day following; for it can not be that a prophet perish out of Jerusalem." When the time came he "set his face stedfastly to go to Jerusalem." The struggle in the garden was only the last act. Every step was a conflict and a temptation, but whenever the time came for the next step, Jesus was ready. The spiritual and redemptive value of his death was not in the quantity of his mental or physical suffering; (that is a caricature of the atonement;) it was in the willingness with which he took on himself this highest and hardest part of his life-work.

The life of Jesus was a life of love and service. At every moment his life was going out toward God and men. His death, then, had the same significance. It was the culmination of his life, its most luminous point, the most dramatic expression of his personality, the consistent assertion of the purpose and law which had ruled him and formed him.

The law under which he lived was the mind and will of God; the purpose for which he lived was the Kingdom of God. Jesus had to learn that law and try out that purpose. He had it within him, but the great experiences of his life brought the will of God and the needs of the Kingdom to his consciousness. The events leading up to his death were of the highest educational importance to his spirit. Here he learned fully the divine attitude toward malignant sin. He entered into that attitude, made it his own, and thus revealed God at the point where the sin of the world and the mind of God were in sharpest antagonism.

He was evidently deeply helped by contemplating the life of the prophets before him. The historical precedents furnished by them took on the significance of a spiritual law to him. He constantly connected his own work with theirs. His mental contact was not with high-priests and kings, but with the men who bore the living God in their hearts and braved the craft of priests or the yell of the mob to speak his word. He taught his disciples to see themselves in the same succession. They were to take opposition as part of their day's work and not mind it. The consciousness of standing with the prophets was so uplifting to him that he made this the culmination of the beatitudes, bidding his followers to rejoice and be exceeding glad if they tasted the same scorn and hate. What the death of Jesus now does for us, the death of the prophets did for him. None of the later theories of the atonement are taught, or even touched, in the sayings of Jesus, except perhaps at the Lord's Supper. The only clear interpretation of his death from his own mind is this, that he ranged his sufferings in line with those of the prophets. This lifts the experiences and functions of the prophets to a very high level in the redemption of mankind.

We said that through his sufferings Jesus came into full understanding of God's attitude toward malignant sin, and adopted it. God's attitude is combined of opposition and love. God has always borne the brunt of human sin while loving us. He too has been gagged and cast out by men. He has borne our sins with a resistance which never yields and yet is always patient. Within human limits Jesus acted as God acts. The non-resistance of Jesus, so far from being a strange or erratic part of his teaching, is an essential part of his conception of life and of his God-consciousness. When we explain it away or belittle it, we prove that our spirit and his do not coalesce.

In the Sanhedrim, in the court of Pilate, amid the jests of the soldiers, Jesus had to live out the Father's mind and spirit. He did it in the combination of stedfastness and patience. The most striking thing in his bearing is his silence. He never yielded an inch, but neither did he strike back, or allow others to do it for him. "If my kingdom were on a level with yours," he said to Pilate, "my followers would fight to protect me." He did not answer force by force, nor anger by anger. If he had, the world at that point would have subdued him and he would have fallen away from God. If he had headed the Galilæans to storm Pilate's castle, he would have been a God-forsaken Christ.

But his attitude was not soft. He resisted. He fought. Even on the cross he fought. He never fought so hard as then. But not with fist or stick on a physical level of brute force, but by the quietness which both maddens and disarms. If he had blustered, he would have been conquered. Christian art has misreported him when it makes him suffer with head down. His head was up and he was in command of the situation.

We have cleared the way for the question, how this obedience unto death affected God. Of course, any attempt to answer this question on the part of any human mind, inspired or uninspired, is an attempt to express more than it can conceive. " God is in heaven, and thou art on earth; therefore let thy words be few." All theories on the atonement prove how unlovely the image of man is when he enlarges it and projects it to the skies. For a Christian man the only sure guide in speaking of God is the mind of Christ. That is our logic and metaphysic.

If we think of God in a human way, it seems as if the death of Jesus must have been a great experience for God. Pantheistic philosophy represents God as coming to consciousness in the spiritual life of men and rising as our race rises. If we believe that he is immanent in the life of humanity and in a fellowship of love with us as our Father, it does not seem too daring to think that our little sorrows and sins might be great sorrows to him, and that our spiritual triumphs might be great joys. What, then, would it mean to God to be in the personality of Jesus and to go through his suffering and death with him? If the principle of forgiving love had not been in the heart of God before, this experience would fix it there. If he had ever thought and felt like the Jewish Jehovah, he would henceforth think and feel as the Father of Jesus Christ. If Christ was the divine Logos — God himself expressing himself — then the experience of the cross reacted directly on the mind of God.

We may conceive the effect of Christ's life and death on God in another way.

As long as humanity lives within the Kingdom of Evil, it is out of spiritual unity and fellowship with God, and

God is forced into an attitude of opposition where he desires to be in an attitude of love and help. Christ was the first to live fully within the consciousness of God and to share his holy and loving will. He drew others into his realization of God so that they too freely loved God and appropriated his will as their own. Thus he set in motion a new beginning of spiritual life within the organized total of the race, and this henceforth pervaded the common life. This was the embryonic beginning of the Kingdom of God within the race. Therewith humanity began to be lifted to a new level of spiritual existence. To God, who sees the end enfolded in the beginning, this initiation of a new humanity was the guarantee of its potential perfection.

This would alter the relation between God and humanity from antagonism to co-operative unity of will; not by a legal transaction, but by the presence of a new and decisive factor embodied in the racial life which affected its spiritual value and potency. When men would learn to understand and love God; and when God could by anticipation see his own life appropriated by men, God and men would enter into spiritual solidarity, and this would be the only effective reconciliation.[1]

In this change of relations Christ would be the initiator. His obedience would be the germinal cell from which the new organism would grow. His place within it would be unique. But his aim and effort would be to make himself not unique, but to become "the first-born among many brethren."

[1] This line of thought in substance follows Schleiermacher.

But what place does his death hold in this process of reconciliation? No place apart from his life, his life-purpose, and the development and expression of his personality; a very great place as the effective completion of his life. Men were coming into fellowship with the Father before his death happened, and before they knew that it was to happen. Jesus labored to unite men with God without referring to his death. If he had lived for thirty years longer, he would have formed a great society of those who shared his conception and religious realization of God, and this would have been that nucleus of a new humanity which would change the relation of God to humanity. Indeed, we can conceive that in thirty years of additional life Jesus could have put the imprint of his mind much more clearly on the movement of Christianity, and protected it from the profound distortions to which it was subjected. There would have been an ample element of prophetic suffering without physical death. Death came by the wickedness of men.

But taken in connection with his life, as the inevitable climax of his prophetic career, his death had an essential place in his work of establishing solidarity and reconciliation between God and man. It was his supreme act of opposition to sin; not even the fear or the pangs of death could make him yield anything of what God had given him to hold. It was the supreme act, also, of obedience to God, to which he was moved by love to God and loyalty to his Kingdom. Moreover, as we shall see, his power to assimilate others to his God-consciousness and to gather a new humanity, was influenced by his death, and the creation of such an effective nucleus is essential to any real reconciliation.

This conception is free from the artificial and immoral elements inherent in all forensic and governmental interpretations of the atonement. It begins with the solidarity between God and Christ, and proceeds to the solidarity between God and mankind. It deals with social and religious realities. It connects the idea of reconciliation and the idea of the Kingdom of God. It does not dispense with the moral effort of men and the moral renewal of social life but absolutely demands both. It furnishes a mystic basis for the social revolution. It would be a theological conception which the social gospel could utilize and enforce.

Finally we must inquire how the atonement affected men. What did the death of Christ add to his life in the way of reconciling, and redemptive power? The answer to this can not be narrowed down to a single influence. An event like the death of Jesus influences human thought and feeling in many ways. I shall mention three.

First: It was the conclusive demonstration of the power of sin in humanity. I can not contemplate the force and malignancy of the six social and racial sins which converged on Jesus without a deep sense of the enormous power of evil in the world and of the bitter task before those who make up the cutting edge of the Kingdom of God. In various ways this realization comes to all who think of the cross of Christ. But the solidaristic interpretation of the killing power of sin is by far the most impressive.   The cross forever puts a question-mark alongside of any easy treatment of sin.

Now, the surest way to make sin pall on us is to watch it go its full length.   The first beginnings of drink, vice, or war are of exciting interest, but the fourth and fifth act make us very sick.   If realistic art would only be faithful and tell the whole story to the end, preachers might suspend business.   An evening out; a broken girl; a shamed family; a syphilitic baby; scrophulous bodies for several generations.   Show us the last results at the beginning and we should sober up.

Moreover, the moral cure worked by sin is most effective in some way when we see our sin working in another life.   A man may be willing to gamble with his own life and take the risk of his sport, but he may shrink from making another life pay for it by agony or death,— provided he realizes the connection.   Therefore it is the business of all who profit by sin to make the exploited sinner forget the social effects of his sin.   The more innocent and lovable the victim, the more poignant the remorse when we realize what we have done.

When discussing the problem of suffering, (Chapter XV), we made the point that pain in the physical organism has a beneficent preventive use and purpose, and that social suffering serves the same purpose for society, provided it can be effectively brought home, and provided there is enough sense of sympathy and solidarity to care.

From all these points of view the suffering of Christ is an incomparable demonstration of sin.   Here we see human sin in its mature and social form; the victim has not contributed to it, so that the guilt can not be divided, palliated, or shifted; the one who suffered was loving and lovable beyond all others; yet great social forces combined with the utmost energy to kill him.

As soon as the passion of the moment subsided and the " interests " were safe again, men were impressed with the innocence of Jesus.   The more they realized the holiness of his life, the strength of his love, the divine value of his person, the more would they feel the sinfulness of the sin committed there.   Besides, the blame was not confined to those who did the act; all the interpretations of the Church emphasized the universality of the guilt.   Every Christian has had his eye fixed on the cross as a place of engrossing interest.   Whatever the theories of the atonement might be, was the death of Jesus not bound to produce a deeper moral earnestness of life, a wider sense of sin, and more self-restraint and thoughtfulness?

Suffering is Nature's publicity method to secure attention to something that is wrong.   All history demonstrates that men are stupid and callous to suffering, even to their own suffering, and that only the most effective means will arouse them to put a preventive stop to what is destroying them.   In all reverence I would say that the cross of Christ was the most tremendous publicity success in the history of mankind.   No event in history has received such earnest and constant attention.   None has spread so much seriousness, and made men realize the sin of humanity from so many angles.   None has so impressed them with their own complicity in it and the solidarity of humanity in sin.

In so far as a genuine consciousness of sin is the first

step toward redemption from sin, the cross was an essential part of the redemptive process. The life of Christ never spread such a realization of sin as his death has done.

Second: the death of Christ was the supreme revelation of love.

Love is the social instinct of the race. In all its many forms it binds man to man. Every real improvement of society gives love a freer chance. Every genuine progress must be preceded by a new capitalization of love.[1]

Jesus put love to the front in his teaching. He was ready to accept love for God and man as a valid equivalent for the customary religious and ethical duties. His own character and action are redolent of virile and energetic love.

If Jesus had died a natural death, posterity would still treasure his teaching, coupled with the commentary of his life, as the most beautiful exposition of love. But its effectiveness was greatly increased by his death. Death has a strange power over the human imagination and memory. A pathetic or heroic death wins a place for a weak and cowardly man. If a significant death is added to a brave and self-sacrificing life, the effect is great. A righteous man might well pray for this as the last great blessing of his life, that his death might interpret the higher meaning of his life and weld all his

[1] The social importance of the Christian doctrine of love is treated somewhat fully in my little book, " Dare We Be Christians? " (Pilgrim Press.)

labors into one by the flame of suffering. This crowning grace was given to Jesus. His death underscored all he said on love. It put the red seal of sincerity on his words. "Greater love hath no man than that he give his life for his friends." Unless he gives it for his enemies too.

The human value of his love was translated into higher terms by the belief that Christ revealed and expressed the heart and mind of God. If Christ stood for saving pity and tender mercy and love that seeks the lost, then God must be that kind of a God. It is a question if the teaching of Jesus alone could have made that the common faith of millions. His death effectively made God a God of love to the simplest soul, and that has transformed the meaning of the universe and the whole outlook of the race. Surely the character of the God a man worships reacts on the man. Suppose that our life has mocked our creed of love a thousand times; how many times would our life have mocked at love if love were not in our creed? Suppose the dualism of the first century had written pessimism and ascetic resignation into our creed. Suppose that instead of the Father of Jesus Christ we had a God who embodied the doctrine of the survival of the fit, the rule of the strong, and the suppression of the weak, how would that have affected the spiritual character of Western civilization? How much chance would there have been for democracy? Instead of that, love has been written into the character of God and into the ethical duty of man; not only common love, but self-sacrificing love. And it was the death of Christ which furnished the chief guarantee for the *on the writing of scripture?*

love of God and the chief incentive to self-sacrificing love in men.

It is true that the self-sacrifice generated by Christianity has been misdirected and used up for nothing in ascetic Christianity. But no one can well deny that the sum total of self-sacrifice evoked by Christianity has been and is enormous, and that its influence on the development of Christian civilization has been very great. Some of the legal conceptions of the atonement have obscured the love of God in the death of Christ. But the fact that the Christian consciousness has reacted against any despotic elements in the character of God, is proof of the fact that the essentially Christian idea had done its work in us and overcome the sinful alloy with which it was mixed.

Since we live in the fellowship of a God of love, we are living in a realm of grace as friends and sons of God. We do not have to earn all we get by producing merit. We live on grace and what we do is slight compared with what is done for us.

This conviction, too, is based on the death of Christ. Belief in the atonement has enabled religious souls first to break away from self-made righteousness and to realize salvation as a gift. With their eye on the cross of Christ they denied the merit system, first of Judaism, later of the Catholic Church. The great religious characters are those who escaped from themselves and learned to depend on God,— Paul, Augustine, Saint Francis, Tauler on whom Luther fed, Luther himself.

Self-earned righteousness and pride in self are the

marks of religious individualism. Humility is the capacity to realize that we count for little in ourselves and must take our place in a larger fellowship of life. Therefore humility and dependence on grace are social virtues.

The cross is the monumental fact telling of grace and inviting repentance and humility.

Thus the death of Christ was the conclusive and effective expression of the love of Jesus Christ for God and man, and his complete devotion to the Kingdom of God. The more his personality was understood to be the full and complete expression of the character of God, the more did his death become the assurance and guarantee that God loves us, forgives us, and is willing to do all things to save us.

It is the business of theologians and preachers to make the atonement effective in producing the characteristic of love in Christian men and women. If it does not assimilate them to the mind of Christ it has missed its purpose. We can either be saved by non-ethical sacramental methods, or by absorbing the moral character of Jesus into our own character. Let every man judge which is the salvation he wants.

The social gospel is based on the belief that love is the only true working principle of human society. It teaches that the Kingdom of Evil has thrust love aside and employed force, because love will support only a fraternal distribution of property and power, while force will support exploitation and oppression. If love is the fundamental quality in God, it must be part of the con-

stitution of humanity.   Then it can not be impossible
to found society on love.   The atonement is the symbol
and basis of a new social order.

Third: the death of Christ has reinforced prophetic
religion.[1]

Historical criticism has performed an inestimable service to true religion by clearing up the historical antagonism between priest and prophet in the Old Testament,
and labeling the literary documents of Jewish religion
according to the religious interest which produced or re-
edited them.   This antagonism is a permanent element
in the Christian religion, and part of the conflict between
the Kingdom of God and the Kingdom of Evil.   A comprehension of the difference between prophet and priest
is essential to a clear understanding of Jesus and to intelligent discipleship.

The priest is the religious professional.   He performs
religious functions which others are not allowed to perform.   It is therefore to his interest to deny the right
of free access to God, and to interpose himself and his
ceremonial between the common man and God.   He
has an interest in representing God as remote, liable to
anger, jealous of his rights, and quick to punish, because this gives importance to the ritual methods of pla-
cating God which the priest alone can handle.   It is
essential to the priestly interest to establish a monopoly of
rights and functions for his group.   He is all for authority, and in some form or other he is always a

---

[1] The importance of prophecy within the Christian religion has
been discussed in part in Chapter XVI.

spokesman of that authority and shares its influence. Doctrine and history as he teaches it, establish a *jure divino* institution of his order, which is transmitted either by physical descent, as in the Aaronic priesthood, or by spiritual descent through some form of exclusive ordination, as in the Catholic priesthood. As history invariably contradicts his claims, he frequently tampers with history by Deuteronomic codes or Pseudo-Isidorian Decretals, in order to secure precedents and the weight of antiquity. He is opposed to free historical investigation because this tears open the protective web of idealized history and doctrine which he has woven about him. He is the middle man of religion, and like other middlemen he is sincerely convinced that he is necessary for the good of humanity and that religion would perish without him. But underneath all is the selfish interest of his class, which exploits religion.

The prophet becomes a prophet by some personal experience of God, which henceforth is the dominant reality of his life. It creates inward convictions which become his message to men. Usually after great inward conflicts and the bursting of priest-made barriers he has discovered the way of access to God, and has found him wonderful,— just, merciful, free. As a result of his own experience he usually becomes the constitutional enemy of priestly religion, the scorner of sacrificial and ritual doings, a voice of doubt about the doctrines and the literature which shelter the priest. He too is a middle-man, but he wants no monopoly. His highest desire is to have all men share what he has experienced. If his own caste or people claim special privileges as a

divinely descended caste or a chosen people, he is always
for some expansion of religious rights, for a crossing of
boundaries and a larger unity.   His interest is in freedom, reality, immediateness,— the reverse of the priestly
interest.   His religious experience often gives a profound
quickening to his social consciousness, an unusual sense
of the value of life and a strong compassion with the
suffering and weak, and therefore a keen feeling for
human rights and indignation against injustice.   He has
a religious conviction that God is against oppression and
on the side of the weak.[1]

The religion of the priest and the religion of the
prophet grow side by side, on the same national soil and
from the same historic convictions, but they are two distinct and antagonistic religions.   The usual distinctions
which separate religions and denominations are trivial
compared with this.   This difference cuts across most
other lines of cleavage.   Since the Reformation, however, the personal qualities which marked the prophet
have become to some extent the mark and foundation of
continuous religious bodies.   Over against Catholicism,
Protestantism has, in its noblest periods, had prophetic
quality; over against the Established Churches the Free
Churches have a prophetic mission.   But the flame of
prophetic religion is always dying down for lack of oxygen.   It burns only when there is something worth
burning for.   It kindles wherever the Kingdom of God

---

[1] I wish to call attention in advance to a book which is still in
preparation, "Religion, its Prophets and its Exploiters," by
Professor James Bishop Thomas, Ph.D., of the University of the
South.   It presents with impressive clearness the historic antagonism between priest and prophet.

is clashing with the Kingdom of Evil. You can tell where the conflict is on today when you hear the voice of prophetic religion. In every religious body, even in those that have repudiated priestliness, you have the undeveloped and unconscious priest and prophet side by side; mixed types, like Ezekiel and Savonarola; embryonic prophets; spent prophets; prophets who have given up; prophets whose bodies and minds have been hurt and thrown out of equilibrium. God knows his own.

The prophet is always the predestined advance agent of the Kingdom of God. His religion flings him as a fighter and protester against the Kingdom of Evil. His sense of justice, compassion, and solidarity sends him into tasks which would be too perilous for others. It connects him with oppressed social classes as their leader. He bears their risk and contempt. As he tries to rally the moral and religious forces of society, he encounters derelict and frozen religion, and the selfish and conservative interest of the classes which exploit religion. He tries to arouse institutional religion from the inside, or he pounds it from the outside. This puts him in the position of a heretic, a free thinker, an enemy of religion, an atheist. Probably no prophet escaped without bearing some such name. His opposition to social injustice arouses the same kind of antagonism from those who profit by it. How far these interests will go in their methods of suppressing the prophets depends on their power and their needs. I have been impressed with the fact that though Christianity began in a renascence of prophetism, scarcely any personality who bears the marks of the prophet can be found in Church History between

A. D. 100 and A. D. 1200.   Two main explanations suggest themselves: that their own capacity for self-sacrifice led the potential prophets into the monasteries and put them under monastic obedience; and that the Catholic Church, which embodies the priestly principles, suffocated the nascent prophets by its spiritual authority and the physical force it could command.

In this way the death of Jesus has taken personal hold on countless religious souls.   It has set them free from the fear of pain and the fear of men, and given them a certain finishing quality of strength.   It has inspired courage and defiance of evil, and sent men on lost hopes. The cross of Christ put God's approval on the sacrificial impulse in the hearts of the brave, and dignified it by connecting it with one of the central dogmas of our faith. The cross has become the motive and the method of noble personalities.

It has compelled reflection on the value of the prophets for the progress of humanity.   What might have been a sporadic and unaccountable religious instinct, has been lifted to the level of a law of history and religion.

By the light of burning heretics Christ's bleeding feet I track,
Toiling up new Calvaries ever with the cross that turns not
    back.
And these mounts of anguish number how each generation
    learned
One new word of that grand Credo which in prophet-hearts
    hath burned
Since the first man stood God-conquered with his face to
    heaven upturned.[1]

[1] From James Russell Lowell's "Present Crisis."   This poem is the finest expression I know of the historic function of prophethood within the solidarity of mankind and its spiritual progress.

The death of Jesus was the clearest and most conspicuous case of prophetic suffering. It shed its own clarity across all other, less perfect cases, and interpreted their moral dignity and religious significance. His death comforted and supported all who bore prophetic suffering by the consciousness that they were "bearing the marks of the Lord Jesus" and were carrying on what he had borne. The prophet is always more or less cast out by society and profoundly lonely and homeless; consequently he reaches out for companionship, for a tribal solidarity of his own, and a chieftainship of the spirit to which he can give his loyalty and from which he can gather strength. Then it is his rightful comfort to remember that Jesus has suffered before him.

Thus the cross of Christ contributes to strengthen the power of prophetic religion, and therewith the redemptive forces of the Kingdom of God. Before the Reformation the prophet had only a precarious foothold within the Church and no right to live outside of it. The rise of free religion and political democracy has given him a field and a task. The era of prophetic and democratic Christianity has just begun. This concerns the social gospel, for the social gospel is the voice of prophecy in modern life.